Changing My Relationship Status

Maximizing My Love Life at any Stage

KRISTEN BLACK

ISBN: 9780999547502

Book Cover By: DesignsbyMia
Cover Heart Image By: BoroBoro/Shutterstock

This Book is dedicated to God; who has and will continue to be my guiding light, my strength and my first love.

To my mother, family, supportive friends, coworkers and all the beautiful souls who have allowed me the freedom to create this written expression of purpose; I appreciate and love you.

Thank You!

Contents

Preface

Wow, now that I have your attention I want to shed light on the title of this book and why I chose it. Initially, I struggled with the selected title because this book speaks a lot about singleness. I believe a whole single person, one who is well rounded and self-aware, is the perfect candidate for a fulfilling relationship. As a professional coach for women, who also specializes in relationship restoration, I am often asked, "how can you give relationship advice to someone when you're not even in a relationship"? A good question from a surface perspective, but the reality, as well as my truth is... every relationship consists of two individuals. It takes willingness from each person involved to do the self-work necessary, on their own, to maximize any relationship. In couples counseling or coaching I challenge my clients to focus on themselves and identify their contribution to the problems in the relationship. I lead them to assess how their choices aid in the errors they face? What can they do differently to enhance the vitality of the relationship and how can they contribute to its healing; factoring in the desires and needs of their partner in the process.

If both individuals are broken, secretly fighting unresolved issues, or simply aren't prepared, it becomes difficult to have a valuable connection with their partner who too battles or avoids their own set of problems. This makes expectations of having a fulfilling relationship (without doing the work) grim at best. Although I am single, I have been in several relationships and that reality has been my biggest takeaway. This is why I wrote this book. It speaks to women; single, dating, and even married, challenging them to dig deep and do the work necessary. The work it takes to maximize their singleness, prepare for a fulfilling relationship, attract positive people and potential partners and even become a better spouse. To achieve this, the work must be done. Doing so will make them a practical contributor to their marriage, promoting the peace, clarity and unity within to enhance their love life.

It is my belief that a broken single woman

becomes a broken wife and oh my goodness, how difficult it is to navigate the very basics of a relationship as a broken person. This is a recipe for disaster. When you're broken it becomes even more difficult to recognize who you are. Now take that and combine it with the expectation we put on our partners to "recognize who we are" and imagine how difficult that would be for them when we often don't even know ourselves. That's tough, and a demanding task might I add, but it happens daily. Today, people establish relationships on the premise of lust alone, often mistaken as love, without the mental and emotional preparedness to sustain a valuable relationship. Without doing the work, they fall prey to the idea they created in their head as it relates to what a relationship looks like. This disconnect transpires because the idea often falls short of practicality, leading to unnecessary tension and failed expectations.

This is why *Changing My Relationship Status* is an important read. It challenges perspectives as well as existing mindsets. It introduces new ideas, data, and even resources to help you better identify yourself so you can thrive in any relationship status. If you're no longer single, this book takes you back to your single self; the woman you were prior to any of your relationships. Truth be told, it all starts there; who you are at the core of you. Without a man, a relationship, children, your career... who you are? Did you know the views and perspectives you hold or held in your singleness truly colors how you engage in your relationships? So no matter where you are romantically, this book is beneficial. Some ideas and information in this book as it relates to singles, encourages fun and excitement in your life. It provides a life-giving perspective that is attractive, bringing the right people into your life. For those who are in committed relationships or married, *Changing My Relationship Status* helps you maintain your identity after the 'I do's'.

I am a believer that developing good habits and practices as a single woman emboldens those same behaviors in long term relationships. In this book we are changing our relationship status from _____Insert Relationship Status and discontent, to happily _____Insert Relationship Status, opening our minds to attract healthy relationships all around. It is my hope that you continue this read with flexible thinking, a willingness to self-reflect, and an active engagement in doing the work.

P.S. - I have also included biblical references for those of you who find it beneficial as well as other resources. Happy reading and enjoy!

The Introduction

Where I First Began

I began writing this book at 25 years old. At that time, I would have described myself as an African American woman, no kids, good job, non-profit founder, and educated with both a Bachelors and Master's degree, yet single! A moral woman, with a clear value system, domesticated even, and single. You get my drift? I would often think "what in the world is going on with me"? I'd spend countless hours on my knees asking God why am I here? I considered myself a worthy woman (and I'm not being biased, I have friends and family who'd back me on this one), with decency, a seeker of knowledge and truth, and dedicated to service. I can cook my socks off, just to toot my horn a little (come on, it's ok to toot your own horn a time or two) but at this point in my life I could not understand for the life of me why the universe saw fit for me to be alone. Fast-forwarding to age 27, I would have described myself the same way but during those two years I did things differently. You see I was accustomed to placing blame for the things that happened in my life. My singleness was not immune. I'd blame my relationship status on my ex's, who scarred me, the independence of the women in my family, and the lack of men in my city to name a few. While all of that deflection served me until age 25, one day it clicked, placing blame wasn't going to bring me a man nor did it do anything to satisfy my soul. I needed my soul to be satisfied; and even if God did send the man of my dreams after my most recent all-night prayer session, would my soul be satisfied? If the women in my family were more dependent, or if there were a bunch of eligible bachelors in Atlanta, would the depths of me be content? Ah ha, it was at that moment I hit a brick wall. The only way to get the answers necessary for these questions was to search within. I had to turn the tides. I needed to look in the mirror and be honest with myself about what I saw. I had to strip naked, physically, mentally and spiritually to examine the root of my thoughts, the founding of my beliefs and the damage to my heart; and it was then I realized there was some serious work to do.

Work, yes work... W.O.R.K. and how exactly was I supposed to do all of that, I questioned? How long would it take? Would I be opening Pandora's Box facing realities I wasn't prepared to deal with at that time? Would I indeed be setting myself back time-wise or up for failure? Did I go too far this time? All of these questions began to invade my mind, and I quickly became overwhelmed. It was as if I had reached a fork in the road. I did have a choice though. I could continue the path I'd been accustomed to, hoping for a different result or try a new technique, chart the territory unknown, to potentially discover new things and possibly love as well. After going through a long drawn out inner debate, I chose the unfamiliar path. I decided to do the work and the work included me, sitting down before my Creator seeking insight about the woman I had become. It was me, on a quest to experience myself from an unbiased vantage point. I wanted to know how God saw me and compare that visual to the way I'd seen myself for so long. Furthermore, I was curious of how others saw me.

In order to sort this entire ordeal out, I started with the simplest method I knew: classic pen and paper. I decided to jot down a few questions to assist me in exploring issues related to my character, attitude, finances, ability to commit, values, my mouth, beliefs, and past relationships. I figured I'd start there and incorporate more areas as they came. I labeled it the foundation of my work and immediately began the edifying process of this lifelong learning.

I received my first learning lesson not too long after starting the work. It was foolish of me to think I could complete such a task in just a few days, but I did. I soon realized that 25 years of life could not be figured out in a week, especially if I wanted my discoveries and lessons to stick. How old are you? Think about trying to solve all of those years' problems in just seven days? Jovial but impossible! For me I was in a desperate place in 2012 but I refused to live in that type of desperation in the coming year. I decided to do what I thought was best and aligned myself with the Creator so He could show me, ME. At the moment it sounded like a good idea but a few weeks in I was convinced I had made yet another mistake. I use the word mistake but honestly, I just wasn't ready for what was to come. I remember the first few weeks being full of ah ha moments and deep revelations.

By the time week seven came around I was tired of being slapped in the face with the real me and not to mention I was still lonely and tired of being by myself. Oh, and if I thought I had seen peaks and valleys in my past, I had no idea what a true peak and valley really looked like. During those early stages of the process I experienced an emotional rollercoaster like none other. The work I started at 25 would not be able to sustain me, but that truth didn't surface until much later! Furthermore, it became very clear over the months that followed that this work would include constant bouts of self-tests, assessments, and learning opportunities. I fell completely off target when I figured this "showing me of myself" process would only take a few days, two weeks at the most. I believed that would be ample time for God to tell me what I needed to do to get this show the road. After hearing His voice, I figured I would immediately comply and by late spring, early summer 2012, I should be getting me a new boo to try this newly refined Kristen on. Well my time line went out the window when God went silent for about three months after that. If I was going to commit to this process I had to develop patience if I desired results. Moreover, if I wanted a good man, I had better stayed focused. So, I rolled my sleeves back, threw on my big girl panties and kept going.

Why am I telling you all of this? Because I don't want you to get in over your head or have unrealistic expectations regarding this process. Oh course I want you to finish strong but I also want to paint a realistic image of concepts you may have never considered. I'm not suggesting that your process will mirror mine, but I am preparing you, if you will, for a process indeed and the process rarely goes as we expect. Nonetheless, if we remain diligent, the process always serves us well.

Let's Continue:

Then it hit me in the head like a ton of bricks when God finally spoke and told me that my singleness, horrible past relationships, and lonely dark place I had been experiencing was a direct result of my negligence. Say what now, Jesus? I literally wanted to give up at that moment because I needed specifics and He said no more. I remember thinking "it took you about 3 months to speak and that's all you gone say"?

I dreaded the idea of traveling down the destructive road of my past to dig up and uproot the mentality and motives associated with my mistakes. I had been so accustomed to traveling down that road for condemnation, but this time I was doing it for exploration and correction. To assess what I could have done better and why I made the choices I made. I intended to put those lessons into a growth collage and move on with my life. Even with my hesitancy and fear, I decided if that's what it took I knew I had to do it. I was so desperate for the truth. I put my little hurt feelings aside and asked God to guide my digging; I dug without reprieve until December of 2013. I really wanted to be a better woman and live my life in a way that was both pleasing to Him and fulfilling to myself. I wanted to be a wife one day and channel that desire correctly this time. I knew that in order to be the best woman I could be for my "one day" family and best wife I could be for my "one day" husband, there was a lot of work that needed to be done internally. I refused to go another day living life the way I had been living it. I had finally made the decision to complete my self-discovery in that season and there was no turning back.

2

Single Because of My Past

A Glimpse of my Personal Self-Discovery

Let me tell you a little bit about myself. I was raised in a Christian home. My mother, a single woman, initially lived a very strict religious, (in my opinion over the top) existence. My father made the decision not to be in my life when I was just a few months old. He went on living his life the best way he knew how minus his pursuit of building or establishing a relationship with me. My mother handled his absence like a pro. She effectively explained his dearth to me, leaving me with a sense of peace that I never knew a person could have growing up in a home with an absent father. The view I held of my father was that of any other stranger on the street, a person I did not know and unless that individual made an attempt to get to know me, it took nothing away from me if we never engaged in conversation. I later learned that was not a healthy thought process.

My mom decided to conduct her household in a manner such as this: if it wasn't about God, it simply wasn't! It wasn't going down, it wasn't to be talked about and it wasn't to be done if it was not God approved. This included extra circular activities, some holidays, worldly traditions and all. While my mother later outgrew her very rigid religious beliefs, they were embedded in me and created much inner turmoil between my mind and spirit. I will give my mom this: I admired her because she didn't have random men coming in and out of her house. The same standard she held for us is the standard she held for herself. As I continued to grow it became very real to me that my mom wasn't perfect and struggled in some areas of her faith walk. That discovery was very poignant for me because trying to achieve that level of perfection I thought she and other Christians had, literally paralyzed everything unique about me. It somehow heightened levels of insecurities I had within myself because I felt bad about not wanting to pray three times a day or the fact that I did not like certain gospel songs. I began to feel like I wasn't God's child because I couldn't catch the Holy Ghost, and I didn't know a ghost that was holy and able to be caught.

I wanted to be like the other girls at church who took notes and desired to be there all the time. I'd raise my hand because everybody else did and it had nothing to do with God or me. Can I get an Amen? I was trying hard to be somebody I wasn't which consequently showed up in my adult life and I wasn't even aware of it. I remember as a child looking up to and admiring my mom, nevertheless there was one thing she wasn't that I desperately wanted to be, and that was a wife. Why did I want to be a wife so bad though? When I began exploring that question it bothered me. Prematurely I began studying marriage around 10 years old. I wasn't your average kid at any age. As a matter of fact, I was always a little too mature. So, at age ten I developed my own case studies by analyzing the marriages around me. I studied the individuals I knew who were married, mostly my friend's parents and couples at my church, monitoring their behaviors, language, beliefs, communication and the way they ran their households. I also took advantage of the free martial counseling sessions I could sit in on, while my mother, who was then a minister in the church, would counsel various and assorted people. Some were married and others single but I would attempt to listen in on her sessions as a child and dissect all the marital and relationship problems these couples faced. Now on one hand this served me well as I am now in the counseling arena, so it was a great experience for me professionally, but personally unbeknownst to me at the time this premature exposure would haunt me for the next 15 years. I would perk up at the announcement of marriage conferences at the church and I remember being the only child excited about accompanying my mother to the several women's conferences they had. I had one goal in mind: figure out the kind of woman I needed to be, so I could one day become a wife.

Once again professionally, a great idea but personally it would be to my detriment. Starting at the tender age of ten I wanted to make sure I was well equipped and knowledgeable for my one-day husband, who at the age of 12 I thought I would meet by 18 and by age 21 be married. Heck, I figured I was being responsible by getting a head start! Looking back on those jovial expectations there is no way I could have been married at 21. I didn't start understanding who I was or even challenging myself to be a better person until I was about 24 and that was only on a surface level. Poor imaginary husband; if I had married him at 21 I would have put the man through pure hell, and created such a faulty idea of marriage in both our little minds. It was true, I never considered the process of friendships or even building a relationship I was just very eager to get married. Was marriage the ultimate goal of life? Was I looking for someone to babysit my insecurities? Was I so ready to have sex without feeling guilty that I figured getting married would be the only way I could do it without sinning? Was I trying to compete with others who were married around me? What was up with my obsession? Why was it still haunting me at 25 years old? Why was I feeling inadequate as a single woman? Why was I still single, again? Why did it matter?

This and many more questions raced through my mind as I matriculated through early adulthood and I was determined to get to the bottom of it. Additionally, I was mentally in bondage and struggled heavily with several conflicting thoughts. On one hand, I knew I had not been the "perfect" girl (who is anyway) they say you should be in religious settings or in your grandmothers' kitchen. Plus as a result, I was fully convinced that the decisions made in my past were linked to the negligence God was speaking of and the sole reason why I wasn't in a relationship.

On the other hand, I could not figure out how and why the biggest freaks I knew ended up getting married or got into relationships easily. They too ignored religious teaching and their grandma's advice but somehow their so called "blatant disrespect" seemed to just get overlooked. I didn't get it. Ever had those same thoughts? Despite that, you still couldn't convince me that my past indiscretions weren't connected to my singleness. But the crazy thing is, somewhere deep down in my heart I had this strong feeling that my past wasn't being held against me and there was more to the story I had yet to discover; but my heart was still broken. So, you can imagine the battle that took place between my private thoughts and my heart. Choosing to ignore the latter, I adopted this old defeated, poor pitiful me attitude, clueless and resentful about my singleness. I concluded that being by myself was a result of my past. I could not wrap my mind around what all I needed to do to help clear things up so I could be blessed with an amazing man! I was convinced that all the crazy things I did, the countless relationships I was involved in (meaningful or meaningless) that was outside divine's will, and my blatant disregard for the Creator's design for love and relationships had to be the reason why I was single and discontent. I was living a life of complaining, negative self-talk, and comparing that was spiraling out of control. I would rehearse all the stupid things I did as a reason to get angry at myself because it was more comfortable to beat myself up and remain negative or bitter, than to actually do the work it took to redirect that energy.

To add to the drama, I was disgusted with

the women I knew, whose past was far worse than mine, but somehow found love and a wedding ring. And for a nice container to put it all in, I was frustrated with God because for the life of me I could not figure out one thing He was doing as it related to the love department of Kristen Black. All I could conjure up was that He was either ignoring me, punishing me, or simply didn't care about me; and that was the narrative I chose. I'd also have you to know that in the process I decided to change my life around for "good" this time. To be a better Christian you know. Stop cursing, partying and having sex, (The Big 3) and as a result I really felt that God should have blessed me with a husband, or at least a meaningful relationship for no other reason than good behavior. I soon realized that didn't work either. God wasn't going to do anything for me with those one-sided motives; plus all that abrupt "change for the better" made me miserable as well. I missed going out!

I had to make the decision, if I was going to be serious about completing my self-discovery; I was going to have to focus solely on God and what He had for me and my journey. It was then I made the decision to not go into 2013 with the same mindset I'd held onto for years. I was curious to unveil my negligence and get to the root of my problem. So that year ended and I started the next year off writing this...

Journal Excerpt: 1.1.13

"Lord help me to hold fast to the vision you gave me. Only you can help me advance. I must fulfill my purpose in this life. I pray that you will guide me and order my steps. Help me to be more understanding and a better listener to you. Today was a good day. Lord please give me direction to show me if my desires and dreams are inappropriate. Lord I need you more now than ever, please show up and help me"

It took several failed relationships and a case of severe depression for me to reach this point. It is my hope that you don't let it get there in your life. I hope this book will motivate you to get started today no matter what season you're in. From this point forward in the book, we'll start doing the work. You and I together! I'll take you through my process and incorporate learning moments in between. I hope you can keep up, this will be a bumpy ride but worth it nonetheless.

~Pause Break~

Switching gears a bit, I am of the opinion that our lives represent a book; our personal autobiography played out on pages with each chapter representing a full year. Before we close each chapter, I believe we are all called to do a chapter report, a cumulative summary of the work done in that chapter (aka year). This report will help determine how we wish to proceed on to our next chapter. However, a chapter report can't be done without actual data, stories if you will. We all have things happen in the course of 365 days. In order to have a concise report at the end of the year, we have to be intentional about charting each moment; the good, the bad, and the ugly moments as well to have a concise summary before we begin writing our new chapter. So not only is doing the work necessary, charting each significant moment and engaging in self-reflection along the way is required so that we transition into the next chapter smoothly and with fresh vision!

Given my theory, think back over your chapters. Did you take notes? Remember mental notes can be sketchy because for most of us we can't remember what we ate last Thursday let alone that random act of kindness that happened six months ago. Or what about the ex you hated when you had him, but now he's magically the best man you've ever known... hold on we'll get to him in a minute but you get my drift? Our minds have too much going on to remember seemingly minor details, and if you've lived long enough you've learned that some of our major lessons come from the most obscure moments. Now you ask, "what does all of this have to do with my relationship status"?

Lots! I am of the professional opinion that many single people don't do the work, neither have many married people; hence the reason why marriages today are in the state of emergency they're in. So, to avoid all of that, maximize our singleness, and best prepare for a fulfilling relationship, we must do, you guessed it... the work which includes identifying our areas for growth. Without doing the work, you miss the benefit of learning who you are, discovering what you truly bring to the table, (and I don't mean material or physical assets), what your heart desires, and the type of people you really need in your life. In this book we are going to begin the working process. We will face some truths. We are going to do some soul searching, mirror looking, truth telling and growing, individually so that collectively, we can add value and meaning to everything we're associated with. Along the way I will be sharing a lot of my personal journey. Why? Because I want women to know I'm human too and I am not immune to the struggles we all face. I want to share my story so you can be assured, I in no way think I have it all together. However, I am fully convinced that we can achieve the life we desire as beautiful women inside and out and thrive regardless of our relationship status. We can take the chapter reports from year's pasts to compile learned lessons as well as great moments and use it to work for us as opposed to against us. It is also my belief that we become hot commodity when we do the work and we become fearless. Fearless women who define our own relationship status!

Spoiler Alert

We are about to tackle some tough areas first then we'll get to the fun stuff. I want to go ahead and get the hard talk out of the way, so we can boss up and look at the fun stuff though different lenses. I suggest that you don't skip this next section because it is necessary. Single, dating, or married the next section is for you and explains a lot as it relates to how you view yourself and your partner. I'm going to be real honest with you. You might want to take a stretch, because being uptight during this section might not make it easier. Open your mind and read this section carefully. It's super beneficial and rewarding I promise you!

3

Your Upbringing & Your Relationships

How You Were Raised Plays a Part in This

Ok girls, let me put this out here; initially this part of the book will have you wondering what does any of this have to do with my relationship status and my singleness? I just encourage you to hold on. It will all make sense in the end. I'm a roots person. I believe everything has a root, every action has a root, every reaction has a root, every belief has a root and I even believe that relationship statuses have roots as well. So, bear with me as we travel down to our roots. In this working process I'm going to share some personal accounts of my upbringing and challenge you to assess yours. On my journey of self-discovery, I wanted to go back as far as I could to help understand the root of my singleness and my attitude toward relationships. So I went back to my birth. Yes birth. Naturally, from the moment of birth, we were all faced with a disadvantage. This disadvantage is simply this: being born into a corrupt world. Innately you and I were born into this world and are likely to be influenced by the family, societal, and even spiritual corruption around us; a key constituent in the self-discovery process. Because of this, all of us are where we are today due to nothing specific but more so the general concept that we're all impacted in some form or another by the corruption of this world! The impact of this corruption endows us with the capacity to lie, be selfish, cheat, steal, swindle people, be dishonest, etc. Now with that, the Creator established a system to help guide us along a path of destiny despite the existence of corruption. The system I am speaking of involves our parents and it charges them with a particular mandate. This mandate suggests that parents train their children in the ways of Truth so that when they become older they won't depart from it. The ways of Truth are the very nature of the Creator and are simply put, tools to help you navigate through life. The Truth includes the good in life, how you treat others, how you treat yourself, ways you can engage positively, and your ability to detect what's good and bad in the world; concepts along those lines. These ways are designed to help us find and navigate fulfilled living! The goal is not to control us, manipulate us, or hinder us; it's specifically designed to prepare us to indulge in all of life's greatness in a healthy and whole manner. The only way we can achieve this is through God (Good) who is the opposite of Evil (Corruption).

After being given this mandate, parents or guardians have the liberty to do with that mandate as they will. Regardless of their decision it was and will always be available to them. It's their choice to decide if they are going to guide their children in truth or further cultivate the assignment of corruption in the lives of their children. Our parent's decision concerning this matter largely impacts who we are as women and is heavily linked to our self-discovery. Therefore, if you were raised by parents who made the decision to uphold this mandate you are very much aware of this concept. On the contrary, if your parent(s) decided to disregard the mandate or tailor it in such a way that agrees with them, you may have been introduced to Truth, here or there or not at all which intentionally or not, inclines you to pursue your own path, often not aligned with Truth. Now take heart, even if you were set on a path opposite of Truth you have the natural capacity to discover Truths path, a concept we'll explore soon.

Now this mandate can be easily identified by parents who find value in it. Typically, the parents who find value in Truth were introduced to this mandate at some earlier point in life. If they weren't, somewhere on their journey they figured there had to be a better way than the way they chose, which resulted in them seeking out the mandate I discussed earlier that was put in place for all of us. If you grew up in home grounded in Truth your parents probably did some of the following to fulfill the mandate: made sure you attended church, enrolled you in every youth program possible at the church or the community center, made sure you hung out with sister so and so's kids or other kids whose parents upheld the same mandate and so forth. Now sister so and so's kids were probably the very kids you should not have been hanging out with, but we will let the past stay in the past and forgive our parents attempt at honoring the mandate. You get my drift. By having parents who honored the mandate, the disadvantages associated with sin or corruption became recognizable due to a constant implementation of Truth, moral codes, and values. Despite our parents' greatest efforts and decision to expose us to Truth or not, the ultimate decision lies with us.

Regardless of their decisions in our rearing, it's up to you and I to decide if we will accept Truth or not. However, the exposure to Truth during our youth, establishes a greater likelihood for us to accept Truth in our lives as adults. It is my belief that with an understanding and connectedness to Truth (aka: relating to your spiritual life) we have an advantageous opportunity to embark on the quintessential exploration of true self–discovery on our journey.

On the other hand, if you grew up in a home that found little to no value in Truth, you were raised with a slightly greater disadvantage. This disadvantage left you to find Truth on your own, which isn't impossible, it's just more difficult. Please note the same can occur with children raised in homes where parents upheld the mandate, however, like previously stated, these children were at minimum given the opportunity to glean from Truth which serves as an advantage. Still, in both cases, it's up to the children, once they become adults, to determine if they wish to pursue the path laid out for them. Now if you were born in a home where the mandate was neither discussed nor implemented, don't get discouraged just follow me it will all make sense in a while. Like I said earlier, we are digging down to the root which is always uncomfortable and can sometimes be unclear but the benefit of digging ultimately exposes truth, clarity, and provides us with the resources we need to be better.

I also want to highlight that being raised in a home that valued the mandate does not mean your parents did everything right. Nor does it mean that if your parents decided to disregard the mandate that they did everything wrong. I am just presenting the basic principled blueprint for the benefit of self-discovery. This is also not a blame game. Our parents did the best they knew how with whatever resources, training, or lack thereof they had and to be frank your parents are people too. People who were born just like you and I with the same disadvantages: sin and corruption. Some parents, in their 40's 60's and 80's are still trying to figure this thing out; so we can't attach every failure or disappointment that we experienced to our parents decisions. Nevertheless, we can utilize our experience to aid us in understanding where we are now, how we got there, and what we need to work on!

Let's take a forgiveness break. Reflect on some of the hurtful things from your past that you endured as a result of what your parents did or did not do. For those who grew up without biological parents, include your family members or guardians that raised you. Ask God to help you forgive them. Forgiveness is crucial for self-discovery and a necessary component of the work involved to becoming a better partner. This will not be an instant transformation but acknowledging that you hold unforgiveness is the first step to restoration. I also challenge you to stop reading here if you are really struggling with forgiving your parents or guardians. Take the next few days and earnestly seek a heart of forgiveness and ways to help you understand the importance of forgiving others. Explore spiritual or universal teaching on forgiveness. As a believer in Christ, I explored the way God used His life as the chief conduit of forgiveness to the world and global sacrifice to atone our personal sins. But regardless of your spiritual beliefs ask the Creator (or your Higher Power) to help you incorporate forgiveness into your daily life and practice living in mercy. Little do you know, this has so much to do with your development as a single woman and your strength as a wife! We are going to get to the root of it all throughout this book so if you remain patient and diligent in this read you will begin to expose the truths in your life.

Ok, so if your parents upheld the mandate, as a result of their decision they not only introduced you to Truth, but they also introduced you to hope in something greater than man. Even if our parents were not the best examples, divinity has a way of orchestrating things despite their/our ignorance and establishing purpose in our lives just through basic exposure to Truth. Due to sin, corruption, and/or our own selfish will, we often steer our lives in the direction that feels best to us, a direction that is sometimes away from Truth. The tendency to do this is not abnormal, however the longer we steer in the opposite direction the longer our self-discovery process becomes.

Despite our direct exposure to Truth throughout our rearing, as women we are still confronted with thoughts, actions or beliefs that are contrary to the standard of Truth; but it is still our responsibility to overcome that negativity and that is exactly what we are doing here. Often ignored, but never separated from us, despite our parent's choices, Truth's presence is always with us. We just must be diligent in identifying it, another key point to take along with you as you complete your self-work.

On the other hand, while those who have parents who found minimal to no value in the mandate may have experienced some difficulty developing their awareness of Truth; there is still a probability that their parents may have accepted Truth at some point in their journey. If not, the child could have been exposed to Truth by a believing family member or friend while they were still moldable. This hopeful interference left room for that child to receive the advantage before they entered adulthood, but this type of situation could have ignited some resentment in them because the sudden change of pace initially comes off abrupt and in some instances unnecessary. For example, consider being born to a family that doesn't believe in going to church. All of a sudden, an aunt out of nowhere starts to come and pick you up every Sunday for church. Keep in mind as a child you were used to doing one thing on Sundays so the new routine that you are not accustomed to, could either make you or break you. You could love the opportunity to get out of the house every Sunday or resent the idea because you weren't used to it or wasn't fond of the new routine all together. In the event that a child's parent refused this mandate or no family member shared Truth with them, as they matriculated to their teenage, young adult or even adult years, they were faced with many opportunities to discover Truth on their own. The great news is that there are many adults who were raised by unbelievers who know and have accepted Truth in their lives! The only struggle lies herein: it's just a little harder to accept the concept of Truth after living 14(+) years doing life without being exposed to it. Consequently, the decisions of this teenager or adult will most likely be the result of a mixture of influences. So, the idea of allowing Truth in totality to come into their lives and introduce an unaccustomed lifestyle may seem overwhelming and frankly is often times too much to take on at once.

Could you see yourself in any of those examples? Perhaps some elements of one mixed with another may describe your rearing or perhaps you have a totally different testimony. Regardless, if all, some, or none of that applies to you, it is a great starting point to figure out your own reality as it relates to the Truth also known as your spiritual source. Truth is what will guide you to and through fulfilling relationships.

I hope you were able to put all of that information together, if not it's ok. It may take reading a few times for you to fully grasp the concepts. I know you may be wondering, what in the world does any of this have to do with my love life. If you are feeling this way, remember a major part of your relational development is your willingness to embark on your journey of self-discovery in totality. The information just shared will aid you in that process and serve as a benefit to you as your relationship status changes. This chapter is called my upbringing and my singleness, because before someone is classified as married, they had to be a single person, right? Before a relationship status was even a factor that single person had to be a young adult/teenager, before that, in descending order, an adolescent, child, baby, and embryo. Every embryo is a result of an egg and sperm that has united. This egg and sperm, once united, came from one man and one woman who collectively (sometimes involuntarily) made the decision to produce, nurture, and guide the person who is now reading this book...this is your foundation. I want to be very clear, because of nature, disaster, free will, God's plan etc. some parents did not or weren't able to uphold their end of the bargain by safeguarding the mandate. Nevertheless, on a very basic level, every individual who made the decision to become a parent was called to produce, nurture, and guide their child(ren). Depending on their willingness to comply, heavily influences the person you are today in your relationships. Answer the following questions to further explore your upbringing and your single season.

1. I grew up in a home with parents who understood and implemented the mandate? Yes or No

2. I was aware of the mandate (as discussed in this chapter) issued to my parents concerning me and my siblings? Yes or No

3. From my perspective were my parents good at carrying out the mandate issued by God? Yes or No

4. Overall, I would describe my parents as?_____
_____
_____
_____
_____

5. Do I think the structure of my home was designed for my success? Yes or No (Explain)
_____
_____
_____
_____
_____

6. If not, how has this impacted me and what have I done personally to aid in my own success as an individual?

_____

_____

_____

_____

_____

7. If so, how has this aided in my success as an individual?

_____

_____

_____

_____

8. Do I blame my parents for who I am today? Why or Why not?

_____

_____

_____

_____

9. At what age did I accept Truth or embark upon my own spiritual journey?

_____

_____

_____

_____

_____

10. If I am to become a parent, or if I am a parent, what will I choose (or what am I willing) to do differently in hopes of creating a more balanced life for my own child(ren)?

_____

_____

_____

_____

_____

_____

My Dad & My Singleness

Since we've dissected our upbringing I want to transition into our personal relationships with our parents. Starting off with the father since it's believed that many women battle with daddy issues I figured it would be appropriate. Therefore, we will begin this chapter by exploring our connections with our fathers, the way we view and treat ourselves as a result, and how all that affects our single years. In 2012 I was led to do a blog called Dear Dad as a public letter to my father God. Growing up in a fatherless home I did not realize the power and presence of the Father God who stood in as the spiritual presence of my absent father. In households where there is a physical father (kudos to all the fathers out there) he has the God given order to lead and influence the household. Ideally, in order for the Creator to fulfill His role in any home, the father (parent) has to be willing to submit to the Creator's control. By submitting or complying with His (our spiritual father) direction, this father (our physical father) is openly accepting divine love within, which in return should radiate through him as he fulfills his duties as the head of household and leader in his home. This agreement will bless the entire house, affording everyone the opportunity to experience the original design and predestined love for family through the leader of the physical father. Biblically this truth stands in

Ephesians 5: 21-30

"21 And further, submit to one another out of reverence for Christ.22 For wives, this means submit to your husbands as to the Lord. 23 For a husband is the head of his wife as Christ is the head of the church. He is the Savior of his body, the church.24 As the church submits to Christ, so you wives should submit to your husbands in everything.25 For husbands, this means love your wives, just as Christ loved the church. He gave up his life for her

26 to make her holy and clean, washed by the cleansing of God's word.[b] 27 He did this to present her to himself as a glorious church without a spot or wrinkle or any other blemish. Instead, she will be holy and without fault. 28 In the same way, husbands ought to love their wives as they love their own bodies. For a man who loves his wife actually shows love for himself. 29 No one hates his own body but feeds and cares for it, just as Christ cares for the church. 30 And we are members of his body" NLT.

I also want to make mention there are some amazing fathers who have not mirrored the role just described in their home. This may include but is not limited to fathers of a divorced home. I started out by saying ideally because I understand every father doesn't follow this structure, and just because they don't doesn't mean they were not or are not great men. This is just a biblical outline of fatherhood in which I ascribe to as I determine the type of men I allow into my space.

Given the biblical or ideal guideline, can you see why it is so necessary to date men who understand the divine design for family? Men who accept their role as a man and are eager to fulfill their call as the leader, know their strength comes from something greater than themselves. This type of man is a prime candidate for partnership. Since I had no physical father in my life growing up, I did many things to gain the love, affection, and direction that I missed as an upshot of my father's absence. Initially I neglected God's presence in my life and overlooked the benefits of having Him as my father until I began the journey of self-discovery. Senselessly, I ventured out on a never-ending quest to fill that absence when I had a Father available all along.

During my self-discovery I learned the absence of my father related to my singleness because it colored how I connected with men. We will talk about the search for daddies as women dates later in the book; I just want to make certain that you understand the vitality of a male presence in the home. It is equally necessary to identify the spiritual presence of Truth who may act as the immediate father in the lives of those whose birth or step father passed, remarried, or left. God also acts as the intermediate father in homes where a father is present but has no relationship with God. Have you ever heard the saying "children are on loan to their parents from The Creator"? That is the exact point I am driving home. Before we are born each of us belonged to The Creator. Because children are unable to understand the magnitude of this, He designed it so their earthly parents could fulfill the role as their physical and spiritual guide. These parents do not replace The Creator in our lives, but they serve as the link between us and Him. When we are able to connect to Truth on our own, some say around age twelve or so, our parents not only teach us the things of Truth but they guide us in Truth as well. This transition from child to adolescent/teen does not strip a parent away from honoring their spiritual commitment. Parents and adults are required to model moral and valuable behavior to their children, as well as to others in their sphere of influence. While it is true, fathers serve as a great example to women, creating a prototype of the kind of man they should want or not want. Did you know there are many people who grew up with fathers in the home but wished they weren't there? Did you know some women grew up with fathers who were abusive, degrading, and emotionally unavailable? Everyone's experience with their father is unique and in our attempt to be better we need to equip ourselves with the resources and tools necessary to be better women, so we can pick great partners. Partners that either mirror or are better than our physical fathers. This relationship allows us to experience a fulfilling relationship that ultimately reflects truth!

This is why it is so vital to embark upon the journey of self-discovery, so you can make the necessary adjustments in your life! If you grew up with an absent father I wonder did you, like I, neglect the Father that was there for you all along for several years, God. If so, you can accept Him into your life and trust Him for immediate guidance today. After all, as our Creator He is able to do all that man can do and more. If you had a father but he was unconnected to the Truth, the Father God was and still is available for you to capture those guiding moments and life lessons. Even if you had or still have an active father, a physical father can never replace the Father God in our lives. During infancy and childhood our natural fathers are the only example we are capable of relating to due to our limited understanding. As we grow and develop into independently thinking individuals, teens and adults, we are able to learn and understand the things of Truth and depend on its principles to further mature us into who we were created to be. Our natural fathers' guidance alone will not sustain us as we begin to experience everything our journey has prepared for us. Parents are responsible for training us up in how we should act, behave, and treat others. They also have the responsibility of introducing us to Truth. By seeing how our parent(s)/guardian(s) interact with each other, their peers, and the community, affords us an opportunity to gain knowledge as to how we should or should not behave and act in similar settings. From our parent(s)/guardian(s) example, we begin to develop our own relationship with God depending on Him to shape us into who we need to be as mothers, wives, in our occupation, church/ministry, community, and everyday life. As an adult, you should be able to determine if your parents modeled a great example of family. Careful not to take away from the wonderful things your parent(s)/guardian(s) did, or discredit them for raising you, we must learn to take the good qualities of our parent(s)/guardian(s) and further develop the negative qualities into good ones as we mature as women. If you had a father in the home I am sure you learned many valuable lessons; some vital, some detrimental, some to look out for, and others to avoid. Store those valuable lessons in your memory bank and please keep in mind that all fathers are only human.

The same applies for our mothers or female guardians. We cannot forget that they are people too. They might not have done everything right, said everything in the best manner, or made the right decisions but they did the best their minds knew how to do. Whether they applied little or much effort, honestly that's all they knew to do. We must forgive, we have to heal, we have to take the good with the bad and make better decisions so we won't carry those negative feelings, behaviors, and attitudes into our relationships.

For those who may have grown up in same sex households, had a father who has died or may have been ill during your upbringing, this information is still valuable. All of this relates to your relationship status because it colors how you engage relationally. By getting to the roots of who you are, you can best demonstrate and convey who you are mentally and emotionally. By fleshing out these issues, you can deal with yourself carefully and engage with others who hold the same respect toward you. You cannot be a happily single, married or dating woman, and I'm talking truly happy, if you have deep seated issues you have yet to face.

Daddy Issues

I do want to touch on the topic of daddy issues for a brief moment, before we transition into some more areas for growth. I think it's necessary to recognize this trend during your self-discovery and explore its positive and negative attributes. So, I will start by saying, many single adult women carry the daddy syndrome (DS) into their dating relationships and are unable to put DS in its proper perspective. While we have some women who have daddy issues and others who look for a carbon copy of their daddies in a man, singleness is a time designed to develop you as a person and help you discover the many issues you foster inside, daddy issues and all. There is nothing wrong with using your father as an example for how you want a man to be, however you must understand that a model is just that, a representation. You cannot expect a man to reincarnate the way your daddy acts, thinks, or how he reacts under pressure. Those are some huge shoes to fill that even your daddy can't fit if he was compared to another man's character.

Since I grew up without a physical father, I use the character of Christ and compared it to the characteristics of the men I'm involved with, (a habit I wish I had developed much earlier in life) however I am fully aware those are massive, better yet, impossible shoes to fill. I know that I cannot expect a man that I am dating to be without sin, or cause the storm to cease at the sound of his voice but I can assess his relationship with the Father and attribute that to how he'll relate to me. I measure his level of love and compassion, leadership and other admirable traits of Christ that I long to see in a husband to determine if we're a good fit. I also gage his level of obedience to Truth and similar characteristics, which are the positive side effects of DS. But all that carbon copy, unrealistic expectation stuff is the negative and the very damaging side effects of DS that you do not want to carry with you for the rest of your life. The same concept that applies to the women who have daddy issues, applies to women with trust issues, abandonment issues, and just plain ole issues. Careful not to negate those as real issues, you will need to work on those during your process of self-discovery prior to entering a relationship. If you're already in a relationship or even married it's not too late. Starting now will aid greatly in your relationship. If you have trouble handling your various issues, please identify that as a burden you carry because once involved with someone, you'll eventually present that burden, subconsciously or not, for them to bear as well. That Sis, is an extremely unfair tradeoff.

1. I grew up with or without a father in the home? Yes   No

2. How did this affect me as a teenager and as a woman?_____
_____
_____
_____

3. How has this affected my relationships?_____
_____
_____
_____

4. I would describe my feelings towards my father as?_____
_____
_____
_____

5. Do I expect the men I'm dating to be like my father, better than my father, or less than my father & Why?_____
_____
_____
_____
_____

6.I would describe my relationship with my father as_____.

7. If I do the following I can mend/improve my relationship or my feelings towards my father._____
_____
_____
_____

8. If I were to be honest, I wish my father was more_____.

9. Does this desire expressed in "Question 8" affect my romantic relationships? Am I on guard against or do I search for this trait in the men I date?_____
_____
_____
_____

10. If I am honest with myself, is it true that I have daddy-issues? _____If so, have I carried my issues into my relationships?_____

11. If so, in what ways have a carried DS into my relationships (good or bad)?

_____

_____

_____

_____

_____

12. Have I accepted God as my father? Why or why not?_____

_____

_____

_____

_____

_____

_____

My Mom & My Singleness

While discussing single women, most people highlight their relationship with their fathers. To go along with the masses, I chose to begin our conversation in a similar fashion, exploring how a woman's relationship with her father affects her life and how that impacts her personal relationships. In our society the idea that a woman's relationship with her father carries the most weight and has a major influence on her future relationships is a very true notion, but I believe how a woman relates to both parents have equal bearing. So, in my attempt to go against popular opinion, I will venture to make this statement: The relationship between a woman and her mother truly shapes her existence as a woman. For those who grew up without a mother, replace the word mother with the female (if one was present) who acted as your guardian. If you were raised in a single home in which your guardian was a male, continue to read this section. Information as it pertains to how you relate to men will still be discussed despite the absence of a female presence in your rearing.

We already talked about the role of a man in the home which is the leader, next we will talk about the woman's role in the home. I want to be sure to add this, as a budding femininity myself (not extreme but I definitely value a few feminist principles) I thoroughly understand that the word "role" can be off putting. Yet, in conjunction with my female empowerment mantra, I am very much a woman of order. Largely in part because I believe it drives down chaos. In order to achieve this goal, I have learned that the implementation of roles are most advantageous when they are clearly defined yet fluid. In this context the word fluid represents the liberty to flow as needed. So as we travel up to this "roles" conversation, I am sure you already know or have heard what a woman's role is. Her role is almost equivalent to female slander in our society but my goal is that after our discussion you will have a new perspective of a woman's influence in the home. The foundational stimulus of a woman in a home, with an active husband is to submit and be a help meet. Ahh, the word submission, a verbal death to a woman's ears, I know, but please hear me out before you start getting too upset.

As women, we have to visualize the strengths of things, especially words, first before we attach negative connotations, unless the word is absolutely negative in its intent. The intent of the word submission here is beneficial and was intended by the Creator to serve as our incomparable power. Have you noticed my repetitive use of the word submission? My hope is that you get real comfortable with that word as a woman whose desires a healthy romantic relationship. Truthfully the word submission can be unsettling because it means trusting in someone else's leadership. While that is a daunting thought in most instances, in order to achieve healthy relationship there has to be an identified level of trust in our partner to do what's best for the relationship. Taking it a step further, as a single woman it is necessary that you understand submission because it is your responsibility to submit to Truth in your singleness. Once you get married you take on double duty (submission to both Truth and your spouse). Single ladies: there is no need to continue wondering how you can submit to Truth during your singleness. I have a few answers to get you started. We submit to Truth by trusting His leadership and doing what is required of us by Him which ultimately makes Him proud. But hold tight, these requirements not only please Him but they serve you as well. Submitting to Truth is understanding that He will never require anything of us that would degrade, demoralize, or devalue who we are to Him, the Kingdom, and to this world. When you become married to a man led by Truth, you as the wife are called to submit to him, in which your husband is to hold up the same standard as God concerning you.

Ladies, our mothers were created to show us the ropes of this womanhood thing. I do not care who wants to argue with me about this next statement or not but I am strongly convinced of it, and I will suggest before you turn your nose up that you hear me out completely. Regardless if you love your mom to death, or can't stand her there is something about you or your personality that mirrors your mother. This is also a huge part of the self-discovery process, admitting and exploring traits that you possess that mirror your mom! I am unsure if you've recognized it or not or have already figured it out and have worked hard at changing that part about you or have fully embraced it; but something you do, some ways you think, or the insistence of your heart can be found somewhere in your mother.

On the flip side there are some things about our mothers that we cannot stand so we work hard at doing the opposite because we do not want to be like our mothers in that area. Either way some elements of your character, the way you communicate, the way you view certain topics, your relationship with the Creator, the way you view men or some other area in your life is slightly, if not all the way influenced by your mother or female guardian. I say that to say this, the way you witnessed your mother or even the women in your life interact with men has impacted the way you interact with men as well. If your relationship with your mother is/was strong chances are you truly look(ed) up to her. Depending on how your mother interacts with men in a romantic sense; her husband, boyfriend, etc. typically reflect how you will relate to men romantically as well. If your mother understood submission, chances are if you truly have a strong connection with your mother you will or have developed an attitude of submission with your one day or current spouse.

Conversely, if your mother did not understand submission chances are you will have to be or have been positively influenced as it relates to appropriate submission to fully carry it out in your home. Please note: I said if your mother understood submission. Submitting is not being a doormat, or a punching bag. Submission does not withstand verbal or physical abuse. By understanding how we submit to Truth as previously explained, is the kind of submission I am talking about. The kind that lifts instead of tears down. However, if your relationship is strained with your mother or if you don't agree with the way your mother chose or even still chooses to submit, you may be resentful and even turned off by the idea of submission within itself. Even if you saw your mother practice submission, you may decide not to submit and vice versa. Nevertheless, the relationship you have with you mother, colors your behaviors, thoughts, and beliefs as a woman in some way.

If your mother did not raise you, take everything just discussed and relate it to the most influential woman in your life growing up. If you grew up with resentment towards your mom that too colors how you interact and engage as a woman, and believe it or not that ultimately influences you in partnership. If you were raised by a single woman like me your views on submission are typically that of your mother, guardian, or the women in your family. Your relationship with Truth and its principles has the capacity to transform your perspective and positively develop your understanding of submission.

For those of you who may have had same sex households, a mother who has passed away or may have been ill during your upbringing this information is still valuable. All of this relates to your relationship status because it influences how you engage relationally. By getting to the roots of who you are, you can best demonstrate and express yourself mentally and emotionally. By fleshing out these issues, you can deal with yourself carefully and surround yourself with others who hold the same respect towards you. You cannot be a happily single, married or dating woman, and I'm talking truly happy, if you have deep seated issues you have yet to face.

1. I grew up with a mother or positive female guardian? Yes or No
   If not, how has that impacted me? _____
   _____
   _____
   _____
   _____

2. My feelings towards my mother or female guardian can be described as?

_____

_____

_____

_____

3. I am similar to my mother/female guardian in this way?_____

_____

_____

_____

4. I am different from my mother/ female guardian in this way?_____

_____

_____

5. My mother and I have a healthy or unhealthy relationship and why? _____

_____

_____

_____

6. When it comes to my mother/female guardian I have to establish these types of boundaries?

_____

_____

_____

_____

7. My mother/ female guardian was a good example of the type of woman I wish to be?

_____

_____

_____

_____

8. I currently experience these issues with my mother or female guardian? SN: These issues can range from major to minor.

_____

_____

_____

_____

_____

_____

_____

9. These issues shape/impact who I am as a woman in this way?

_____

_____

_____

_____

10. My relationship with my mother has positively or negatively affected my relationships in the past & how?_____

_____

_____

_____

Disclaimer:

The section "Your Upbringing and Your Singleness" comes from a very traditional standpoint. I have not done enough research to speak confidently on same sex parents and how that dynamic impacts women. The entire purpose of this section was to dig deep and dust off our foundations. Our foundation is really the key component to our relationship status. When our foundations are not secure as single women we take that brokenness with us as we begin to construct a foundation with another individual. **Please do not skip this portion.** It's necessary Sis. It will help you discover and uncover some pertinent things about you that will help you heal and maximize your love life. You deserve a healthy one!

NOW TO THE FUN STUFF

4

Why Me

Because I'm Totally Confused on This One

After discovering where I stood with my parents and how it really said more about me than what I said about myself, I still had questions. I know earlier on, before we got all deep and stuff, I did a lot of talking about getting past certain moments in my journey... but how did I do it? That's the topic we're transitioning to now. I've already told you about the countless number of times I've asked God why me, to the point that it's not even funny, but I also know many women who are guilty of doing the same thing too. After all the blaming, self-loathing, and attempting to figure things out on our own, we often get to that point as women, why me? Perhaps it's not the blatant "God, Why me" prayer but it could show up in the whispers of your private thoughts. Or while you're at dinner with other couples and you're the only single one there. What about when you scroll past happy couples on social media and the idea finds a way to pop up. Just maybe! You then begin to ask yourself or the Universe what's really going on, all to have a list of ideas rummaging your brain as to why you're that discontent woman in the first place. Quite frankly that process can be beyond frustrating... until now.

Now, we're going to do it. We're going to face this thing head on and pick through some of those thoughts in an attempt to answer the "Why Me" question. (Insert yourself here) Have you ever felt like this: Like out of all the women in the world why am I a 19, 25, 32, 46, or 65 year old single woman? Or this: "What did I do so wrong to land me this plight"? "Could it be that I've just had sex with too many people"? "Or is it that God is punishing me"? Or: "What about Jason, poor Jason that boy loved me to death and I treated him so bad...is this karma"? His name may not be Jason but if you can relate you know who your Jason is. "Maybe God doesn't like me; you know I was a rebellious child" you wonder. Or this one: "What about that time I stole my best friend's boyfriend in the 6th grade"?... Oh no I got it: "It's because I'm cursed... no woman in my family is happily married"? Or you take it here: "Who is out here working against me... someone, somewhere has to be hating on me something vicious"; and this relentless quest instigates more questions and eventually spirals out of control! Then it happens! We torture ourselves by digging up our past using condemnation instead of correction which ultimately works against us. We bring up all our failures and demean ourselves in the process in an effort to carnally explain something that's spiritually divine.

Have you been here? Sitting around wondering and trying to come up with all the reasons you think you could be single, alone, by yourself, unhappy, without a hand to hold, or a real man to call your own. I say this tongue in cheek but the truth is, depending on where you are in life, this could be a very harsh reality and if you're too afraid to admit it I will be the first to tell you, I have done this to myself countless times pre, post and during the work. I end up feeling defeated and several steps behind as I gave the enemy a hand up in beating me down. One of the scriptures I love is "who can understand the mind of God"? Trying to figure out why you're single is a clear example of you trying to understand God's mind. But in my mind as a single woman it was justifiable because the truth is, my background isn't squeaky clean. I've done my fair share of dirt. No, I haven't treated everyone like I wanted to be treated. Yes, I've neglected God for a man a few times! Sure, I belong to a family primarily of single women and if there's a charge I'm sure I'd be guilty. Or what about those of you who did everything right. You held your virginity, been extremely selective about who you date, you've maintained a consistent relationship with God, and some of you have even been married before all to have it end in a bitter divorce. You did everything right and you still have the same question...why me?

So, you can see how easy it is to fall into this trap. Your past elicits destructive thoughts, and those thoughts beget other thoughts that don't serve you and the only way to escape this is to change the narrative. You can change the story you tell yourself. Once I got this revelation I began working on thoughts that profited me. But there was one stipulation; these thoughts had to be realistic. Anything made up or fantasy would only assist me temporally and I needed a long-lasting narrative that could sustain me in my season. I had to really ask myself, what does any of those rummaging thoughts, real or imagined, have to do with my current relationship status? By choosing to not place blame on others or even myself, I came to conclude that the answer was: NOTHING! As far as my relationship status is concerned there was no connection. However, the lessons I was intended to learn from the circumstance of my life had EVERYTHING to do with where I stood relationally.

Are you shocked? Well so was I because I justified my negative thinking to the books I've read about karma. In some instances I found it easy to blame others for where I was relationally. But the reality was it's not their fault. God saw fit you to be where you are today, in your current relationship status, because there is something for you in it. Social media expert's advice about why you're single and how you need to learn a thing or two from such and such because she has a man, can toy with your mind if you allow it. Or how women raised by single moms can't treat a man, her main reason for not having one they say. These are also frequently the same people who claim that women raised by both parents have greater odds. But there's no way these blanket statements can be true for everyone all of the time. If so, every woman raised by a single mother would be single and every woman with daddy issues would have lousy husbands. I have girlfriends who were raised by both parents who've met horrible men too, so the situation we were given, or our personal indiscretions committed can't solely be to blame.

Yes, we all know karma is real, but it doesn't always show up the same way it was given. Is there any validity to those teachings often used as scare tactics such as, you reap what you sow (that's in the Bible), and fatherless girls can't properly love a man because she's never seen it demonstrated in her home? Sure, I believe those notions are applicable on an as needs basis but like we discussed earlier, the facts are: every woman that was raised by her mother is not single just as every woman who struggles with daddy issues, doesn't have a man in her life who resembles her father. Now there are lessons to heed from both backgrounds and that's our takeaway.

Yet, where you are right now is so much deeper than what you did in the past or who was present or absent in your home. Just as I've met many women who were raised with both mother and father that are still single, have suffered a nasty divorce, are currently in a hellacious relationship, or are a part of a loveless marriage. I have also met women who were raised only by their mother and have the values of God running through their veins. They are married to amazing men, have great boyfriends, and actually enjoy their singleness. So if *Part I* is true: Women without father figures are singe then *Part II* has to be true as well: Women with father figures are married or in relationships. Simply put, neither is always the case.

We must wake up as women and stop letting the self-inflicted accusations and humanistic perspectives bring us down! Personally speaking, I believe all those worldly notions if not fully dissected can serve as distractions to get your focus off the main thing. Switch your outlook to useful techniques about how you can get the love you deserve, as opposed to rehearsing useless explanations as to why you're single.

This one thing you can be sure of, when it's your time girl, it's your time. You can go and get you a man today. You sure can! You can walk into any super market, convenience store, or even down the street and I guarantee there will be a man somewhere waiting on you, ready to commit their lives to you and give you everything they have, or don't have; but is that what you really want? We will revisit this idea later in the book but let that thought linger around as we continue. I'll go ahead and tell you now.... that's not what you want! No way. So be patient, there is a lot of work to be done and in this book, we will talk about it all. Your past, present and future, your family, friendships, choices... beliefs, sex, money and ex's too, you name it. We're going to discuss it and we're going to prepare you for not only what you desire but what you deserve.

Now you may be wondering "will any of this "work" explain why I'm single Kristen". Honestly Sis, it will if you let it! I hope you find the missing pieces to your puzzle in this book and not only begin but complete the process of elevating yourself. I hope you can locate the gaps in your story and begin the bridging process. I pray you receive the necessary revelation and determination to work out your kinks. It is my hope that you remain diligent in this read and don't give up now. So, the next time you wonder "Why Me" don't go for the jugular. Don't place blame all over the place, it won't help you.

I'm going to be real frank Sis as I introduce a new narrative and I'm asking that you brace yourself because initially it may seem like a hard hit but I promise its eye opening. You Ready? The reason why you're single is because it's not your time! As I sit on my couch at this very moment writing this book I type each letter as a single woman myself. That overarching response is just as real for me as it is for you. It's not our time and before you totally freak out, truly think about how awful it would be to get something right now that's out of season.

Out of Season Relationships

Be honest, when it relates to any other area in your life you turn your nose up to anything out of season. Let's say you see a young lady walking down the street with a double-knit sweater, some leather pants, and thigh high boots in 100 degree weather. What would you say? "Now, she knows she wrong for that"! "I know she's hot"! "She knows she could have waited until it got cold outside, she's crazy." Something along those lines. Or what about getting a watermelon in the middle of winter? Upon purchase you think to yourself, this is probably a bad idea. Once you take it home, cut it open and taste it, you say to yourself, "I knew this was a bad idea, I should have waited"? Why because the outfit and the fruit are out of season and when it's out of season we look out of place, we feel uncomfortable, it tastes bad, and it's often a waste of our time, energy and resources.

Those same emotions are the direct result of being in a relationship out of season. How dreadful would it be to end up with a guy who leaves a bad taste in your mouth? You know he's the wrong one so you're super uncomfortable, you feel out of place as it relates to where you should be in life, and you waste your time, energy and resources on something that was never designed for you in the first place. So, ladies once again I'll be the first to admit it, the reason why you and I are currently single is because it's not our time. But hold on, as we continue we'll discuss things to consider and tools to use during this season so we'll be best prepared for a fulfilling relationship. If you're in a relationship hold on we'll get to you too. These tools are designed to help us best work on ourselves so that we can present the best version of ourselves to the person God really has for us.

Oh, and I'd have you to know, when I got the revelation in 2013 that God was not punishing me for my past everything began to make sense. Thank goodness, because my past was a mess and there was no way around that. Now, my new narrative matches the truth as to who I truly am beneath the surface and yours will too. I was so relieved that God was not holding singleness over my head as a penalty for my previous indiscretions but it took more than just changing the narrative for me to get "It Right". I needed to continue the work.

I have some good news. The same truth applies to you today. If you were raised in a strict Christian home that truth can be hard to accept when "Bible Thumpers" attempt to terrorize you into thinking that your life's misery is a result of your current and past sins; and how could you retort that notion... it seems believable right? And to their defense a portion of that is the truth. Life is indeed a series of cause and effect so the result of a thing is linked to a previous action. For example, if you speed you put yourself at risk of getting a speeding ticket. If you got a speeding ticket, then chances are you were speeding. But not everyone who speeds gets a ticket. Ah hah, here is the lesson. If you got punished for every inaction you committed you'd be in deep kimchee. So, while the notion that perhaps your life will be better if you stop sinning altogether and made better decisions is a great idea, it in totality is impossible. No one is perfect all the time. And while I think that idea is the best advice you'll ever receive, I also believe there are tangible ways to live realistic lives and adopt different perspectives that adds health to your journey. One perspective is, there are times and seasons where you could be doing everything right and life still finds a way to go wrong. How is this perspective healthy? It gets you out of this unrealistic mindset that if I consistently make good choices I am automatically guaranteed to receive everything I want out of life exactly the way I want it. While our goal is to always do our best in order to maximize this life and the life to come, doing everything right "ain't gonna guarantee you no husband" or anything else you really want to happen. Nor will it make your husband change his mind about you or act better. It's when preparation meets the divine plan that you get what's best for you and it always happens in God's timing. You can get something you want alright, and it could be one of the worst things that have happened to you. Can you relate? If not, I know you know or have heard of that wife or girlfriend who, had gone through or is currently experiencing unshakable feelings of disdain towards her partner, yet she got what she prayed for. Think about it!

Moving on let's look at my brother Job. One thing I love about the Bible is that it is a book of not only what to do but what not to do. If you don't believe in the Bible, please don't disregard this section or even this book. I am sure there are other publications, books, movies, etc. that you don't necessarily believe in such as magic or people flying on objects, but you've entertained them nonetheless. So try not to give up now, just hang tight. (insert smile) Anyway, the Bible is full of positive insight, cautionary tales, and life-giving alternatives. It has some major mess ups and successes, romance, death, and the list continues. Personally, I think the entire book has been falsely coined a book of rules but I for one believe that is so far from the truth. The reason why the Bible is so pivotal to me is because it served as a reference guide during my work. I relied on it heavily along with other publications to truly get to the core of me in the process. I must say the revelations gathered stabilized me. So as a result, I want to share with you a little story about Mr. Job.

If you've never read about Job he was a stellar individual. He was an upright man with extreme wealth and lived as a true believer of God. One-day Job was minding his own business and received the craziest news of his life. All of his ten children were dead, on the same day at the same time. Wow! Then he lost all of his money and to top that off, he got really sick with a painful illness for a very long time. The story ends beautifully but during the process Job went through several painful chapters that his "sins" or past had nothing to do with. He was experiencing some necessary seasons in his life that made absolutely no sense to him. There are countless other examples of good people who experienced hell, yet their hell had nothing to do with anything they did in the past. While some of you may not be experiencing a painful illness or loneliness, being single for a great length of time can bring about a sense of pain. However, just like Job, your past choices may not be the primary constituent. If you haven't forgiven yourself it's easy to feel like everything else is holding you in contempt as well, but that's not the truth.

One of the beautiful things I love about being in relationship with the Creator is that as a direct result of me accepting Him, He's cleared my past from my record and has given me everything I need to move forward. It is because of this relationship I am confident that my sins, past mistakes and failures are cast in the sea of forgetfulness and are wiped clean. Taking it a step further, my past has a purpose. Good or bad it was necessary and it served as a catalyst to help me transition into the woman I am today. Get it? Your past has purpose!

For each of us there are lessons that need to be learned in our time of singleness so that we won't repeat the same mistakes, failures, or sins as we continue forward. During your singleness and or alone time it's much easier to make change without the external factors to distract you. Be it your crazy work schedule, for my work-a-holics, children, responsibilities, or even relationships, they all have the tendency to occupy time and energy that could be reserved for self-reflection. Self-reflective work often takes the back burner the more demanding or piled up your obligation and sometimes distractions become. Whenever you feel isolated or alone that's a good time to do some self-work. I did the work, not to get a man (to attract good men, yes) but more so to be a better person and live life maximizing my moments and every opportunity.

5

The Comparison Trap

But Why Does She Deserve a Good Relationship

L ook I'm just going to be real and cover all the bases. If you're too ashamed to admit this has crossed your mind or truthfully, you've never thought about this, we're going to talk about it anyway. It may help you better understand someone you know. Comparison is the enemy of originality and our singleness just seems like the opportune time to start swooning over all the people around us who are in relationships. Even if you're in a relationship, relationship envy can be real for you too. Listen up Sis, don't do it! It's an emotionally draining trap that ultimately gets you nowhere. But just in case comparison is your thing or your struggle, we're going to do a little exercise to break things down a bit. Think about all the individuals you know who are in relationships. Do you think just because they're currently in a relationship, they are ready to be in one? I'll give you a second to think about it but I think the answer is going to shock you. The answer is yes, they absolutely deserve that relationship! Was that a shocker for you? Well let's look at this beyond the surface. The fact that someone is "ready" can mean a variety of things and I want you to take an honest assessment of their relationships, in totality, and ask yourself this question, "how much do I actually know about their relationship" and "is their relationship the type of relationship I truly desire"?

If you don't know the answer to these questions because you don't know much about their relationship, other than they look happy, then it's safe to say you really don't know what's going on in that relationship. In that case it's technically not worth your time even wondering "why is she in a relationship"? You know nothing about it. Next let's take a relationship where you get bits and pieces about it from social media sites or social settings. Because you get to see moments of them here or there, the moments they chose to show by the way, please understand it's still bits and pieces so your assumptions have no bearing on the truth; this too is not worthy of comparison. On the contrary, let say you know something about a relationship and everything you know is super jacked up. You know it's jacked up too. That relationship where the woman always looks unhappy or complains, crying to you about her never ending relationship issues. Yep, you've met that person. Why are you even comparing yourself to someone who's trying to achieve stability in dysfunction? Is it because she has a warm body to go to bed with every night... that you know of? If that's the case have a slumber party if that's what you're missing.

My mom once told me if you want a person's life you must take the whole story. You can't say "dang I wish I was in a relationship like such and such, but I want my man to come home at night". No sweetie if you want such and such's relationship, get ready for your relationship to involve a man just like the one such and such is dealing with. A man who does not come home at night or does whatever he desires without any consideration of you. Let that sink in and while no relationship is perfect, you know when something isn't right so don't play yourself, you're too smart for that.

Lastly, let's say you do know the story and it's great. How awesome is that, an example of true love. As women we should celebrate the success of families and relationships across the globe. We really need as many examples as we can get of pure love instead of the images that perpetuate the negative stereotype, that the only thing that's left in the big ole world is trifling men and women. Stable relationships provide hope, at least for me, and hope heals the world. You know a true sign that you're ready for a relationship? It is when you can purely celebrate others when they get in one.

So back to our original question, what makes them "ready" for a relationship? I have a few ideas for you to consider:

1) **They have mastered the art of self and have something besides their body to offer.** Let me explain. Men love a confident woman. She knows her body is not her greatest asset, she's direct, upfront, and honest about who she is and takes no prisoners. Men, not adult boys, find that truly attractive and her authenticity has landed her an amazing man. This woman is truly ready for all that God has for her in regard to love.

2) **She is "ready" to learn some lessons.** Actually, I'm not sure how ready she is but life was determined to teach her some so...voila... she's in a relationship full of lessons. Some women are currently in relationships with men never intended for their lives but due to their stubbornness or naivety, they are in a relationship with a man designed to teach them many lessons. Whatever the lesson is, I'd venture to say I'm not sure if I want to know the details and I pray for them because when we're forced to learn a divine lesson, due to

stubbornness, eagerness, neglect, etc. it leaves lasting results, <u>LASTING</u>!

3) **She was "ready" to connect with a man who equally was not as ready.** What does this mean: Here we have a woman who is not ready to be in a relationship. She meets a man who is not ready for a relationship either but both individuals in their heart of hearts believes they are, so they go for it despite their unpreparedness. They willingly dived into a waterless, concrete pool, head first, hand in hand, because they were "ready". Clearly, they survived, you see them, heck you even know them, but their bruises, pain and internal damage can sometimes be lifelong. How does that sound? How does it sound to get with a man where the both of you aren't ready and consequently suffer unnecessarily as a result of willfulness? In the natural, this relationship classically looks like two people who meet and instantly have this passion filled connection. She knows little about him, except for what he's willing to

share and he only knows the information she's chosen to divulge, which all could be a fictional fantasy of who they both wish to become in their minds or in their reality. The truth is to be determined with time but their eagerness and passion filled connection causes them to move too soon. They fall deep and hard and after only a short while, usually 3-6 months, they realize they are horrible for each other. However due to stubbornness they continue to go through the motions, which could last for years, because they both made this willful decision. Willful people would rather side with arrogance and endure intense pain, physically, emotionally, and even spiritually than to declare their humanness, even if it's to themselves, and risk leading a more fulfilling life! In relationships this typically looks like an unhealthy soul connection where one broken individual is trying to fix another fragmented person when they're barely capable of holding themselves up. Not to mention their innate tenacity to work really hard in an effort to mold the other person into what they want them to be but haven't mastered how to construct their own life. What a task. What a relationship!

So the next time you're tempted to compare or wonder if "two people are ready for a relationship" you know the answer. It's definitely a "Yep, they sure are" and a "Nope, I'm ok with my portion because the only story I'm privy to is my own"! I don't want to be the woman ready for some tender lessons because I refuse to take heed from the signs of life. I want to live my best life, receiving all the good things precisely designed for me and no one else.

This life is a journey full of signs and direction. For some, signs come in the form of visions, words of wisdom, internal instincts, the words or actions of others, the way life orchestrates itself, and several other unexpected ways. Pay attention to the signs and be observant. Most significantly, be careful what you wish for because when you get it you may realize that you've bitten off more than you can chew. In some instances it's more than you wish to chew if you know what I'm saying. So be

thankful for your portion and your lot in life...
it's all divine.

6

Why They Say You're Single

Unveiling Societal Opinions

Wrapping your head around being single at any age when you desire a relationship is a frustrating thing. Plain and simple, you can't understand for the life of you why you're single and the truth that it's not your time is unsettling. You look around and your friends, (personal and social media alike) are getting married, engaged, or simply getting into a relationship for crying out loud and it makes you feel weird inside. For some that feeling is anger, or dis-ease, for others it's jealousy or envy and you don't know who to be honest with about your feelings! For some you can't even be honest with yourself but your late night thoughts tell the truth. Your silent tears speak volumes of where you are and your private conversations with yourself or your most trusted friend bares it all so....

Ready or Not...Let's Go

For my girls in relationships, don't skip this! You know single women and perhaps even your own views as it relates to singleness may be challenged. Your perspective and let's be honest your relationship status may even change, and you want to be prepared regardless. So, ladies, starting with the obvious, the most common societal opinions are: All good men are taken. Or what about this one: women outnumber men by 3, 6, 12, or 112. Let me think of another one...no one is looking for commitment anymore, I live in the wrong city, I probably should get out more, I met my husband...he's married, and lastly, it's hard to tell who's down low and who's not. Yes ladies, I've heard all this and more and if I were to be honest I too have said most of these things as well. Now the down low part is difficult to detect, hence the saying down low...too slow, I've had to honestly ask myself "are most of these statements accurate"? As it relates to a few I've faced the music, identified them as true and moved on; but taking a deeper, more intuitive assessment, I added another element to the original question and made it more personal: "does any of that matter concerning my situation" and definitively the answer was "truthfully" they don't!

You get it ladies? Sure, there are hard facts, statements, beliefs, you name it, floating around about us single girls, trying to explain exactly why we are indeed "alone" but none of that matters concerning you and your situation unless you allow it. Let's start there and let that sink in! This truth, can absolutely apply to many challenging areas in your life! What is for you is already yours it's just waiting on the ok from God to be released to you. It's like that perfect black dress that's been in your closet for years. It's already yours but you're waiting on the right, might I add unknown, time to put it on. While the thought, "at least I can see my dress; I have no idea what my future partner even looks like" may cross your mind, regardless if you can see the dress or not, it isn't until you wear it that it means something. Until then it's simply holding space in your closet until you're ready to put it on. Just like your future partner, if predestined, he's in his holding place waiting until you're ready.

What a humbling truth and if I were to get all the way real with you, I'd admit my own struggles with that truth. Personally, I used to get super offended when people told me I wasn't ready for a relationship. I would respond, verbally or mentally with something like "Who are you; crazy married lady or immature single woman to tell me that I am not ready". Followed by a "You weren't ready when you got married and still aren't" but then deity began to work on me. I tell you, in moments like these it takes a God blow to put me in my place because humanly speaking I don't care about your pedigree, education, spiritual relationship or perfect relationship(s); none of that means anything to me and my life if my spirit doesn't agree with where you're trying to lead me (that could be physically, in conversation, any prophecies, etc.). So yes, girl that statement "you're just not ready for a relationship" would and still has the capacity to boil my blood (depending on the messenger) because logically I don't think the intent of others is always pure.

The pure intent however behind saying a woman is not ready for a relationship does hold several truths. Let's look at a few!

1) **Who you are today is not ready for the man your future husband is at this moment.** What does that mean? Let's explore! Your divine husband maybe currently in his growing process and because of the type of woman you are, the man he is right now during his process, is not insightful enough to pursue a woman of your caliber. Through his process he needs time to become the man he's intended to be for you, and if by any chance you'd get into a relationship with him right now, you would not be ready to or able to handle his shenanigans or his process. Therefore, be thankful that you're being shielded from that one.

2) **You as a woman, right, smack, dab in the middle of your process may not be**

ready for a relationship. Perhaps your struggles with insecurities, which no person should be forced to deal with by the way, or your loose ended relationships, could be hindering the development of an authentic relationship. Possibly there are some areas you could mature in, selfish ways you need to correct, stingy habits that must go and a mean attitude that needs transformation. Perhaps you're still trying to figure out who you really are or you're too religious or self-righteous...and so forth. One or a few of these endless possibilities could be the areas extending your singleness.

3) **God has a different plan for your life.** If you're not ready for a relationship because God has a different plan for your life I cannot even attempt to explain what this means for every reader but here are a few examples to ponder. Let's say an opportunity for you will be opening up in a different state six months from today and your future husband lives there. This

form of "not ready" really has nothing to do with you, per se, or your future husband's need to grow up. It's simply a divine move that is scheduled unbeknownst to you that is not only designed for your career growth but also a linking mechanism between you and your soul mate.

A second example looks like this; let's say marriage isn't in your cards for the next 10, 20, or even 30 years. There are some divinely, advantageously amazing things that must happen in your life that doesn't require romantic partnership, which puts you on reserve (so to speak) until your task or tasks are complete. Then you'll have all the tools necessary to cultivate the romantic aspect of your life you truly deserve. Now, keeping it real that is a tough pill to swallow and as a 30 year old woman that pill appears to be a horse pill but the reality is, what if that is my story. Although that thought occasionally leads me to an open rebuke; I can't help but to think that I maybe rebuking the very fragment of me that's the most significant to my story. Does it diminish the goodness of my Creator and all the wonderful things predestined for me because a man in not written in my storybook until the latter chapters? No, it doesn't but the society we live in makes it hard for us to believe that. So regardless of how long you've been single, who you are, or what you have or have not done, if you're still single at this very moment you're just not ready to be in love for one reason or another, and that readiness can change at any moment. You can begin to attract the right people into your life depending on your willingness to do the work. The work will begin to cultivate healthy relationships in your life; and above anything else, relationally, that should be the ultimate goal.

7

She Can't Even Get a Man

Is There Any Truth to It?

We live in a world where we are defined by our relationship status. As a result, to be accepted, many women seek relationships to be vindicated by society and/ or validated of their worth. During my self-discovery I found I subconsciously yielded myself to that belief. I mean seriously, who wants to be identified as the woman who "can't get a man"? It was a phrase, that somehow masked itself as a trait and was thrown around like leprosy; an idea, if you will, that dooms a woman to singleness and words that plague you to eternal "aloneness". I later questioned if that so-called trait "she can't get a man" held any weight. Like, what does that really mean? "She can't get a man", and who are the people speaking this into the lives of many women? What are they like, what type of relationship are they in? This led me to dissect the descriptive I was so afraid of being identified as. She can't even get a man? What exactly do those words mean? Is the phrase "she can't get a man" a true proclamation for any woman?

When I began to assess the people in relationships around me, the findings were humbling to say the least. To my amazement I discovered that women were able to get into relationships despite being crippled, crazy, diseased, and broken. So, then I began to wonder, what was so obscure about me and any other single woman that labeled us incapable of "getting a man"? I was further led to explore, was any of this a legitimate concern. Was it possible that "she", any woman, could in no way get a man? Absolutely not! This then led me to examine the hearts of those who loosely made those claims? Typically, the individuals who made these references as it related to women were rude, immature, and at the very least uninformed. As I continued to explore this notion deeper I found that it really didn't matter what type of woman you were, anybody could literally get a man. I've seen it with my own eyes. Still there was a real question that needed to be addressed. One that stood out to me like a sore thumb; what was the going definition of a man? Like the going rate for a gallon of milk, I wanted to discover what was the going definition of a man? When people used the phrase, she can't even get a man what exactly was their point of reference? Ha, the answers amused me. Of course, they varied depending on who was asked, but there was an underlying similarity in the response among the people who uttered that dreadful phrase.

The definitions ranged from an individual with a penis, a male who takes care of their responsibilities, a male who worships God; some people describe a man as a male who protects, a male who keeps them company, a male who, and I quote "does what he does because he's a man" and the list continued. Can you guess which of those responses were linked to the people who believe that women are incapable of getting a man? I'll let you decide, but as I was faced with these various definitions, I was led to question my own definition of a man and evaluate the type of men I attracted and were willing to date. Furthermore, I questioned if the men in my past were simply there so that I could avoid that stereotype. On the petty side of me, I also came up with a timely response to that deadly belief "she can't get a man" and that was "so how do you determine what a man is?" In all seriousness though, we must stop identifying ever person with a penis as a man, yes, he is a male human being but manhood is developed, not given.

Are All Single Women the Same

Let's consider the idea that all single women are the same. Are we? Are there certain characteristics that only single women have and if so, am I guilty by social clumping? Are those characteristics the reasons why I'm by myself? As a single woman, often grouped with other singles, are we somehow interwoven by a common thread? Could the common thread be that we're simply without a secure romantic relationship? If that were the case, wouldn't it be that all married women were the same as well? Basically, the question I'm posing is "are all single women created equal" or is it that all single women share similar personalities? I knew in my heart of hearts neither were true but since I was on a journey of self-discovery that knowing wasn't enough for me. I needed facts to back that up.

So, I picked up that pen and paper I had been using and attempted to describe myself to the best of my ability, at that time. I wrote out what I desired in a relationship and how I spent my time as a single woman. For your own journey I challenge you and your single girlfriends to do the same. Yes, married women are welcome to do it as well. Once you've completed it with about 2-4 friends compare your responses. Of course, married women would write down what they desire from their marriage, how they are as a wife, etc. While completing this assignment I realized I was not like any other single women I know and no other single woman I knew was just like anyone else.

Nonetheless, I did notice there were certain actions single women engaged in that could potentially be aiding in their singleness. However, this did not mean there was one single *women's code of conduct,* that single women abided by which limits their ability to attain a relationship. To prove my theory, here are a few areas I found women in general lack control over. Before we get to that, I want to mention the advantage this time of singleness affords us because now is the prime opportunity to generate a plan of action to develop ourselves in the following areas. Those areas are our attitude, personality, personal views, worth, values, and individual motives.

Attitude: Single ladies it's important that we check our attitudes. Our mood swings and PMS bouts are not attractive and could possibly get in the way of meeting a stable man. Additionally, your attitude about being single can be unattractive as well. If you're always complaining about being single, if you're an angry single or even if you speak negatively about the relationship status of others, people can see your unhappiness and decide early on that they want nothing to do with that. Keep this in mind too, I also know some mean, rude and just plain nasty married women but keep in mind our goal is to be the best partner anyone could ask for. After all, we will be held accountable for our actions as a wife when it's all said and done. The same applies to married women. Yes, you may be married and have a bad attitude, but ask yourself this... how is my disposition affecting the morale of my home and my marriage. Negative energy breeds more negativity so be mindful of your attitude regardless of your relationship status.

Personality: As a woman with a strong personality I had to understand that while I see my personality as a strength, in some instances it would be beneficial to scale it back a bit. Having a strong personality, I sometimes come off too aggressive or even intimidating to men. Do you have a strong personality? Conversely, some women have very meek personalities. Meekness can also be unattractive for some men and a field day for others. There are men out there who prey on meek women and you never want to be anyone's prey. Just as there are men who are ready to attack strong women, you don't want to be in an emotionally violent relationship either. There is a healthy balance of both and I think as a single woman it is imperative to find your personality balance. Personality balance is that mixture of assertiveness and humility. Some readers may feel they shouldn't have to change their personality to get a man and I am going to share a little insight with you concerning that. While you shouldn't necessarily have to change your personality, it's always beneficial to work on improving it. I too, once thought I was not being true to myself by modifying my behavior, but I came to understand that maturity is knowing if, when, for how long, and in what way, to do, say, or act. It's that knowledge that makes for a powerful relationship.

Personal Views: Personal views are indeed that, personal; and you are entitled to them but sometimes our personal views may totally conflict with someone else's. As a single woman you must learn to be ok with that, without compromise but full of compassion. I think often, especially if you've been alone for any length of time, women start to alter their personal views to mirror the views of the person they're interested in. Or the complete opposite, hold onto our views without the willingness to even hear another's perspective. For example: let's say you're not an outdoors girl but you meet a guy who enjoys camping. Before you know it, you're embellishing stories about how you truly enjoyed that one camping trip you went on with your play cousins many MANY moons ago, knowing good and well you sat in a tent crying your eyes out and swatting flies. Laugh out loud! This is an example of altering your views in hopes of landing that man. The same can happen with a man who wants to take you camping for the experience. Because you hate outdoors your refuse to budge or even consider alternatives to camping. This also happens with religious views, moral codes, etc. all the time. Knowing when to bend, break, or even alter your personal views is just as crucial as realizing when your personal views just don't mesh with someone else's. When this happens, your willingness to redefine the relationship or let it go altogether, if need be is a true sign of readiness.

Self-Worth: I'm just going to put it out there. There is a wave of women, not just singles, who have no idea of their self-worth. Before they know it, they're doing things, agreeing to stuff, and putting up with things beneath them just to gain male attention or even maintain a relationship. Ladies, know your worth. It's imperative that we know our value beyond our bodies and physical appearance. God has blessed us tremendously with assets that are very appealing to mankind in general, but the woman you are on the inside, your character, work ethic, intelligence, and your spiritual girth, far exceeds anything your body could ever offer. It's vital for you to know that and to be slow to enter relationships as you're mastering that principle.

Personal Values: Single ladies what are your values? Many people know they have values but when asked to identify them they often stumble. It's very necessary that as a single woman you identify your values! Know them, believe them, and carry them in your heart because a relationship should never alter what you believe.

However, over the course of life, values do change. If you were raised in a family oriented household, chances are those values are deeply instilled in you. However, as we journey our own paths we may find ourselves redefining our values, which is a very healthy part of the process. We learn to keep the ones that serve us and redefine the ones that don't. If you grew up without a beneficial value system or with loose moral codes you're not exempt. As an adult woman, you must be intentional about connecting yourself to individuals or groups that are grounded in the values you're attracted to. This will allow you to redefine your value system and incorporate those values that work for you. Not only that, when you're truly determined to elevate your life, you'll benefit tremendously by surrounding yourself with people who uphold similar moral codes and values. You, no longer hang with women who cheat on their spouse if married or have men in and out of their beds. If you want to see change in your life, you must begin making alterations on your part. While some severances may be painful at the time, you'll see the quality of your life increase by separating yourself from toxic individuals and influences.

Motives: Ok this was a very real area for me. When I asked myself this question initially I was stumped? I'll be honest, this took time, purging, redirecting, and seeking for me to become super clear about my motives. I not only sought clarification for myself but for my one-day spouse, children, family, and community as well. I created a list of questions and the one question that really guided me during this process was: What is your motive for being in or desiring a relationship? Honestly, discovering the answer to this question was no walk in the park and it exposed so much about myself that I had to ask the real question, "Do you REALLY want to be in a relationship?" The next step once you figure out your answer is to determine if your response is more self-serving or sacrificial. While a relationship should serve you, it equally, if not more, will require sacrifice. If your motives are more self-serving, you'll benefit from shifting your intent now as opposed to when you get into a relationship. This shift is challenging as a single woman, so can you image the hurdles you'll face in your relationship if you carry this same mindset. I believe the #1 selfish reason to get into a relationship is because you are lonely and the second one is so you won't grow old alone.

During my self-discovery I learned that being in a relationship requires continuous acts of selfless love. Relationships are not always about me, what I want, and how I want it done; it is about the both of us. I had to ask myself if I'm entering the relationship looking out for my own self-interest. Additionally, what was I willing to sacrifice for my partner? Later I'll share the reasons why people should enter into a relationship, but for now we're addressing areas for growth in our singleness on a larger scale. Later in your spare time I encourage you to further explore these concepts more intently.

This next excerpt includes actual journal writings I did in 2014 which highlight my recognized growth in the following areas, since beginning the journey in 2012.

My Personality~ I now monitor and analyze things I do or say to gauge if my actions or words could potentially hurt someone.

My Attitude~ I have begun considering how my feelings affect others around me. I learned it's important to think in cadence with my feelings. How I feel should not affect my day, and it is extremely selfish of me to allow my feelings to impact someone else's day as well.

My Personal Views~ As a strongly opinionated woman, I had to learn that everybody doesn't care to hear my opinion all the time. No matter how "Right" I may think I am about a situation it's not my place to prove my "Rightness" about everything, in every conversation. I have also learned it's important to think first and speak second. Views and opinions are often accompanied with a plethora of feelings. The danger of this is that feelings are extremely fluid. We can experience a good feeling one second and feel like crap before that second is even over. That's why operating on feelings alone can increase the likelihood of making a bad decision. I soon realized that in order to counter that, my personal views had to both evolve in expression and expand in order to avoid that error.

My Worth~ To tell the truth and shame the devil, I talked a good game but for years I had ZERO self-worth. I let men in and out of my life, taking pieces of me with them as if I belonged to them. For years I cared about everyone else but me; and not in a self-pitying way either. I truly cared more about a man's happiness than my own. This mindset led me to relationships with people I KNEW I had no business with. Because I have never been married, it became apparent to me I was accustomed to operating as a wife with men who were not my husband. As a result, by playing "wifey" I sacrificed my morals, beliefs, and even wants to show someone else how worthy they were; failing to determine and even define my own sense of worth.

My Values~ are deeply rooted in the things of God...NOW. For YEARS, my values were a story board of ideas and opinions developed by myself, family, friends, married people, God, and the media. I created my own value system that lacked stability. I was never intentional about establishing my value system according to my personal relationship with God.

My Motives~ Being single affords me the opportunity to examine my motives for wanting to be in a relationship. Over the years I have sought out relationships to fill voids, save me from feeling lonely, satisfy my lustful desires, provide companionship, find someone to consistently talk to, and many other reasons I can't even think of at the moment. My motives for being in a relationship were never to join with a man where we could evolve spiritually and become useful instruments for both the Kingdom and this world. My main concern was to make them happy; even if it included doing something I did not want to do, all in hopes that they would return the favor for my seemingly selfless actions. I never viewed relationships for purpose, a coming together of like people, with the same foundation, seeking to build a legacy for this generation and future generations to come.

In addition to the 6 concepts we discussed, there was one last concept I identified!

My Savior~ is Jesus Christ. For so long I longed for relationships so some man could come in and save me. Save me from being alone, save me from boredom, save me from loneliness, save me from living alone and all these things that should not be sought after from an individual. Being single has proven to be a beautiful thing in my life. It has afforded me many opportunities to prepare for my future family. I have established peace within; I have understood the importance of prayer and relying on God before entering into a relationship or making decisions. I have died to myself so that I can live in the fullness of God. I understand the importance of being led by God and not my feelings or emotions. I chose to make Him proud above all things. I began to understand His love for me and began to believe that He'll never withhold any good thing from me. Only a loving Father would do that and I appreciated Him for it.

8

The Untruth's Of Singleness

What you Don't Have Time to Entertain

One thing I learned during my self-discovery was, the solidity of my foundation developed my resistance to the untruths of this world. In order to do so, let's explore some untruths about being single and determine if and how we've been impacted by them.

Untruth #1 Being single means there is something wrong with you.

I beg to differ. As previously stated, by the mere fact of being alive and breathing there is something wrong with all of us. Single or married we are all inclined, at one point or another, to behave beneath our potential. If undisciplined, this has the capacity to destroy us in our singleness and in our marriages. Now if something is wrong with you in a sense that you talk too much, or smell, have sex way too casually, or don't know how to communicate with people, etc. that doesn't automatically explain why you are not in a relationship. I know many women who smell, don't respect anyone, will cuss a man out in a heartbeat and had sex immediately upon meeting a man, who have active dating lives and/or are married. If you are seeking marriage for the sake of having someone, get married. Anyone can do that, it's not a difficult task as we discussed earlier.

I want to drive this point home because it changed my life. My mother once told me if you can't do anything else you can do one or two things: get married and, unless there is something medically wrong with you, have a baby. It may not be the man you want to be with, but trust me the ugly, the old, or that "corny" man who approaches you all the time will marry you in a heartbeat and gladly put a baby in your stomach. Yuck! Ladies the point of this little vignette is to help you see that many people are getting married but how many people do you know are happy in their marriage? How many people have God's hand in their union? We have no way of knowing what goes on in someone's home unless we live there with them. I will even venture to say that many people live in houses with women (or men) who are getting verbally abused, cheated on, and degraded and have absolutely no clue what's going on. So be careful what you ask for and the people's lives you covet; be content with where you are in life and understand there is nothing specifically wrong with you.

Conversely, if someone has told you that you have body odor, your mouth is foul, your attitude sucks or you have sex with men too soon, then those are clear areas to start working on during your singleness. Other than that, there is something wrong with everyone so don't buy into the hype. Ok? Work on what needs developing and keep it pushing.

Untruth #2 Because you are single proves you can't keep a man.

I know we talked about not being able to get a man, but what about keeping one? Keeping a man is a huge responsibility that even as a married woman I do not wish to have. I refuse to be responsible for keeping anybody except my own child or any children placed under my care. To keep a man suggests that men are undeveloped beings that are unable to care for themselves. In this case it also makes the assumption that every man requires a females' directive on how to manage and attain his basic needs. Let me be the first to say, I do not want a man like that, do you? Even possessing the idea that you are to keep a man identifies an area to work on prior to any relationship. God or the enemy are the only keepers of men, this applies to both men and women. You determine who's the keeper of your soul by examining who you submit to and whose guidance you accept most in your life. Submission, an area we talked about earlier, simply means doing what is requested of you. That which you are submitted to in the spiritual realm is your keeper? So in a sense this 2nd untruth is indeed a truth, since you are single you cannot keep a man because you are not created to keep a man in the first place. Capshe? I know many of us use this term tongue and cheek and I believe that's ok if you really know who's "keeping your man" it's all good.

Untruth #3 Being single means that I am lonely.

What is lonely? The internet defines lonely as "feeling sad, though being without friends or company". Therefore this basically means, unless you have no friends or family you should not embrace the untruth about being lonely. It is unreal to think that feelings of loneliness will not pop up periodically. Expect this to happen, pop up feelings are totally normal. It's determining which ones that'll pop up that is the most difficult. Moreover, it's how you handle those feelings which are even more vital. As you grow in that area you learn how to consistently manage those pop up feelings. However, being lonely should not be a place where you exist. You know that girlfriend (or this could even be you) who always talks about not having anybody, or constantly complains that they are tired of being by themselves even if they are in your company? Yep, you can be sure without a shadow of a doubt this woman has created an existence of loneliness. Let's break down this concept. Existing in the place of lonely, is a trick from the enemy to disperse negativity throughout your life and shackle you to bondage. It allows you to move from appreciation for what you do have to a place where your primary focus is solely on what you do not have. Many single women have loving friends and family who they totally overlook in search of this ideal mate that doesn't even exist in their lives and is highly fantasied! Holding onto this bondage keeps you suffocated by lack, a strong desire to have what you do not. Aside from family and friends the most important part of our lives is our relationship with the Creator. No matter what happens in life, where we are in life, or what we are experiencing, God is with us. How dare we overlook His presence when life gets inconvenient or uncomfortable? While it's easy to acknowledge His presence when we are rescued from a catastrophe, it's not as easy when we are sitting at home on a Friday night watching old reruns alone. Somehow, someway we forget about God's presence then, I wonder how? **Truth Moment**: As best explained by my cousin at a women's luncheon a few years back when you are single you are "A- Lone" a single, (one) person but lonely you should not be. On the other hand, you are free to borrow loneliness but I am certain when I say this, it's not worth the trouble or brain power. In essence, being "A LONE" individual means you are one person, whole, and by yourself. That doesn't sound like the most glamorous thing but I am going to tell you why it's the best news you will ever receive! By being "A Lone" individual you are afforded the priceless opportunity to get your single, self together.

Not single in a literal sense, but figuratively alone means single, like the number one. During this time, you now have the chance to develop as a whole individual. Life has a way of making us all jaded in one way or another and each time something happens to us a piece of our confidence, hope, esteem, and/or faith can be taken away. The very moment something is taken away we automatically feel its effect. This effect directly attacks our emotions causing us to identify with feelings of loneliness, surrounded by a sense of lack or a feeling that something is "missing". Naturally, as a defense mechanism, we try to find things to fill those empty spaces or missing elements in our lives. We often do this to lessen the impact of that void. Does this temporary solution of picking up random pieces to fill our emptiness yield lasting results? Does it ever?

Ladies I want to spend some time on this topic because I believe loneliness is the driving force behind many of the impulsive decisions we make. Please allow me to break down the loneliness and emptiness epidemic. If you are cut and are left with a gash in your skin, you can simply place a band aid on it to cover the damaged part of your skin, right? However, if you do that the damaged part of your skin is not fully restored until the natural skin grows back. Can I ask you what types of band-aids have you been using to cover the damaged areas of your life? Money, men, sex, eating...the list continues. Now it's important that you follow me here so you can get this point in its entirety. Let's explore our natural bodies. Inside each of us, naturally we have a spirit and a flesh this is a natural occurrence. When we experience damaging situations in life it directly affects our flesh (body or our person) and leaves an impression on our soul and spirit. A damaging experience can be a break up, a rape or molestation, death, neglect received from parents or family, etc. As a part of this self-discovery process, take a few minutes to identify the damages in your life. In order to completely restore the damaging parts of us we need a supernatural occurrence to take place so that it can heal. The Spirit, which dwells in us, naturally brings healing but we have to feed and stimulate that part of us in order to profit from it. Here are a few scriptures that support the presence of the spiritual dimension in us to further justify its existence and highlight the war that wages within us.

John 14: 17 NLT

"He is the Holy Spirit, who leads into all truth. The world cannot receive him, because it isn't looking for him and doesn't recognize him. But you know him, because he lives with you now and later will be in you. Jesus said that when I depart from you I will leave my spirit to keep you".

John 14: 23-29. NLT

"Jesus replied, "All who love me will do what I say. My Father will love them, and we will come and make our home with each of them. 24 Anyone who doesn't love me will not obey me. And remember, my words are not my

own. What I am telling you is from the Father who sent me. 25 I am telling you these things now while I am still with you. 26 But when the Father sends the Advocate as my representative—that is, the Holy Spirit—he will teach you everything and will remind you of everything I have told you.27 "I am leaving you with a gift—peace of mind and heart. And the peace I give is a gift the world cannot give. So don't be troubled or afraid. 28 Remember what I told you: I am going away, but I will come back to you again. If you really loved me, you would be happy that I am going to the Father, who is greater than I am. 29 I have told you these things before they happen so that when they do happen, you will believe".

Once we experience something damaging in our lives or in our flesh we need the Spirit to heal us and make us whole again. Did you get that? When there is an empty space in your life, a void, you need a supernatural occurrence to take place so healing can begin. The only way to escape voids, loneliness, and lack is to accept the natural healing process. This natural healing process includes recognizing and accepting the Spirit into your life to make you whole.

Here is a common question as it relates to accepting the Spirit: If I decided to accept and acknowledge the Spirit within, will healing occur instantaneous? This question requires some clarity. As it relates directly to the proposed question the answer is No. You are smart, you know that when you cut yourself it takes time to heal but you are hopeful, and in some instances confident, at some point complete healing will occur. Conversely, although total healing will not begin instantaneously, the healing process will begin immediately. Just as you have faith that your missing skin will eventually grow back, it's equally beneficial to hold that same belief concerning your emptiness. It's imperative to understand that you cannot view singleness as a void because it's not. It is not a part of who you are. Singleness is a necessary season in your life to help you develop into a complete person. During singleness our ultimate desire is to walk in wholeness. When someone is whole there is no inclination of emptiness. Voids or loneliness however, can stem from an individual trying to force an occurrence in their lives that isn't destined to take place at that particular moment, time, or season.

Untruth #4 I will be single forever.
Well, if you keep saying that, yes you will be

even if you get married. Am I saying that a married person can possess a single person's attitude? I sure am. If you are wondering how, I will address the single person first then the married next. Let's begin with the most basic lesson learned during our youth: Words Have Power. The entire world we live in was created by what was said. This is significant as it relates to your singleness. If you continue to say negative things about your love life you will ultimately begin to believe it and what you speak will manifest in your mind. Your actions, thoughts, and body language will give off a certain vibration and that energy will be made available to others, whether you give it permission to or not. You can literally walk into a room and by your actions and even your disposition; others will be able to detect the discontentment you hold as a result of your singleness. Will they know the root of your discontentment? No, but they will be able to sense your temperament.

To counteract this negative persona, stop saying it, stop thinking it, and stop believing it! You will not be single forever, unless you truly believe you will be single forever and then in that case you will be. On the other hand, it may not be God's will for you to be in a marriage. If that is the case be certain that His plan is for your good. Singleness however, should NOT mean without relationships; it just means without marriage. If singleness is yours, own it and cultivate positive relationships with all kinds of people.

Chances are if you're reading this you're more than likely a single woman so use this time now to build authentic relationships, even with members of the opposite sex, people overseas, in your community, as the list really doesn't have to end. Just because you're single doesn't mean you can't produce good, quality relationships. My grandmother adopted through friendship once told me "sometimes it's better to be friends than to get married; essentially you get the same benefits". Coming from a woman married for over 30 years her words resonated with me. Ladies, you cannot manipulate God into bringing you a man any faster because of your poor, pitiful me attitude. Do you really think God's actions are determined by our unstable emotions and wayward feelings? Sis, if you use manipulation with God you are sure to use manipulation in your marriage. Despite what we feel we need, and what we think is best for us, God knows for sure what is best. Place your cares, burdens, worries, and frustrations on Him. He holds your future in His hands and since your future is in His hands, your future is safe!

Next, you may be wondering how can one be single in their marriage? There are many ways a person can be single in a marriage on varying levels. One way a person can be single in a marriage is by doing things secretly and separately from their spouse. Examples may include: making huge purchases without their agreement, accepting gifts and things from adult men and/or women unbeknownst to your spouse, having a separate or secret bank account, etc. People want to be married so badly, but still want to operate as if they are single.

Secondly, a married person can show that they are single by not being "present" in the marriage. Yes, a married person can be "there" physically but not "there" mentally for their spouse so as a result they continue to operate as a single person. Married 'single' people also have this warped sense of security and presence as it relates to their spouse. If their husband is away on business they start feeling like they are alone, not understanding that their marriage was not made on the consensus of having a body there to occupy a space or fill a void, but a heart there to merge as one and fulfill a mission. A third way a woman can be single in a marriage is to marry the wrong man. I hear it all the time from married women, "I feel like I'm in this by myself". What a miserable existence. You think being single is bad, try being married but feeling like you're single. Can we say confusion?

This is why it is imperative that us single folks keep calm during the process and be vigilant as we date and consider who we will partner with in life. What is their character like? How do they relate to their current family? If they're distant and emotionally bankrupt what makes you think they won't be removed and emotionally obsolete in a marriage? So yes, a person can be single forever regardless of their relationship status. All I'm saying is we have to stop borrowing these world premiered reasons as to why we are single. Verbalize instead that you will forever be whole, not single.

Ok now that we've looked at worldly views of single women and have completed some work by being open and honest to determine if the views or perspectives discussed impacted our lives, we can move on. Next on my self-discovery I wanted to assess if there were more personal reasons that impacted my singleness and attitude towards relationships. Before we get to that in the next chapter, answer the questions below concerning your experiences with the "untruths of singleness".

1. Have you been plagued by any of these untruths? _____

_____

_____

2. If so which ones?

_____

_____

_____

_____

3. If not, how were you able to counter the impact of those untruths?_____

_____

_____

_____

_____

_____

4. Do you/Did you once agree with any of those untruths? If so which ones? _____

_____

_____

_____

5. Given the information discussed in this chapter which "untruths" do you have to work on removing from your language, actions, or beliefs?

_____

_____

_____

_____

_____

6. If applicable, which "untruth" will you work on eradicating first or what's a different untruth you've heard and even believed about your relationship status?

_____

_____

_____

_____

_____

_____

9

Defining Singleness

What is it Really?

Given all that information, regardless if a physical father is present or not, the type of relationship you have with your mother, the untruths concerning your relationship status, your past, and everything else combined, one of the common mistakes we make across the board in our singleness is not fully developing our self. By exploring the impact that our current, non-romantic relationships have on our lives is a great starting point. It's said that during our teenage and young adult years we began to establish our identity, but I would venture to say in some cases many mature young adults and even middle-aged adults are still on that quest. Listen, that's not always a bad thing I mean come on; can you honestly say you knew who you were and what you wanted out of life when you graduated high school? I can attest that in high school I had a strong idea but as I have matured that identity I thought I had and that future I thought I wanted at age 18 significantly changed at age 25. I can assure you, due to the nature of the growing and maturing process alone; the things, the people, and the ideas you felt so passionately about in your teens will change, (or has changed) as you develop into the woman you were created to be. I truly believe in some cases God extends our singleness to afford us more time to recognize who He is and learn why we should depend on Him to develop and mature us.

Contrary to popular opinion you cannot change yourself. You can do things differently for a limited amount of time but without divine intervention you will eventually pick up those same negative practices or bad relationship habits. You are a person who has emotions and unless you have consciously decided to not be led by them on a daily basis, some days those feelings will get the best of you. If uncontrolled, our emotions have the tendency to cause us to do things we said we would never do, say things we said we'd no longer say, and a list of other things we've vowed against. That's the futility of creating New Year's resolutions or these abrupt life changes we take on because everyone else is doing it. It takes nothing to create a list of changes that one wishes to make as they enter the New Year or after they've recently experienced a bad break up. However, it takes much more effort to honor those commitments months into the year or weeks after feeling lonely especially when you see no physical change or when a new man hasn't surfaced. Just like our resolutions, without spirit-led direction in our singleness, as soon as we feel the effect of not experiencing a relationship in the near future, we fall back into old habits even self-destructive activities and mindsets.

Since I've gotten that out of the way, I wanted to address my pure feelings, definition, and perceived reason for being single pre-self-discovery and post-self-discovery. Notice how my definition of singleness reflect a more solid description post my self-discovery which I believe not only shifted my outlook but will impact yours as well. I am now going to be vulnerable and share with you what I jotted down.

Feelings, Reason, and Definition Pre Self-Discovery

Feelings about being single: "Ok being single sucks. It's a time in my life where I am by myself and I'm constantly stuck in this undesirable space of wanting to be in a relationship".

Reason why I think women, including myself, are single: "Because there is a shortage of good men or all the good ones are taken. Contrarily, I also believe if a woman is single for too long then God knows she ain't ready so He's waiting on her to get it together".

Definition of singleness: "Being single means being lonely with no one to share my life with."

So those were my initial answers, early on in my quest for self-discovery. During this process I experienced a great awakening (as I'd like to call it) and I want to share with you how my thoughts developed.

My Awakened Definition: "Singleness is an ordained and necessary part of life that is to be experienced by every person living on this earth. This experience is designed to mature and develop every individual into the man or woman God has created them to be".

That's it! That's what being single is all about, that's the reason for it, the definition, the everything you need to know as a single woman. I now challenge you to do the same on a sheet of paper, jot down how you feel, your definition, and your perceived reason for being single? Call up your girlfriends and family members and ask them to do the same.

As you complete this part of the process I also want to reiterate that being a single woman is not your identity, a misguiding idea held by many single women prior to their own self-discovery. Did you know before you were born there was a destiny placed on your life? Yes, you were born to fulfill an extraordinary, especially for you, very specific type task. This task is your sole to-do assignment that needs to be completed before you leave this earth. This task can be one thing or a list of things depending on your destiny. It's up to you to find out what is it and get started. Nobody will make you complete it, but if you're determined enough you'll find your purpose and if you're blessed enough to accomplish it, you are sure to live a gratifying life. Everybody has a different task and just like we have authentic finger prints, we each have authentic destines that are tailor made for us. Your task or purpose speaks more about your identity than your relationship status.

Being single, once again, is the most opportune time to get your SELF together. Your thought pattern, beliefs, values, morals, and attitude to name a few are areas to be developed while you are single. These areas need to be checked and put into perspective daily to ensure both consistency and proficiency. I believe this part of the work needs to be continuous to elevate you into the woman you were created to be. Not some days, not some times, not around your birthday or the first few months of the New Year, but every single day of your life. This is what truly stabilizes you as a single woman.

As a believer in Truth, I trust that my durability can only be found in the Creator as discussed in "the root of your singleness" and Him alone. In today's society we hate absolutes, but the only way to have a sure foundation is absolutely through God (our spiritual life). For me this idea is supported by the evidence of my life. What evidence has your life produced (good or bad) and through it all you're still standing? When there are some people who gave up while you still pushed through or have even died before attaining the same goals you're still pursing or have completed. As a result of my partnership with our God, He has proven to be consistently solid, secure, and stable and has further proven this many times throughout the world. Psalms 18:31 validates this...it explains that He does not change. He is not lead by His emotions nor by the days of the week. He is stable and sure, and the last time I checked nothing permanent holds up on futile or fragile foundations. We have to develop our spiritual lives to steady the foundation in our lives and in our relationships. Check out this except from a blog I did on being single.

Dear Dad,

Being single has been one of the greatest experiences I've had. I never really understood, valued, or respected being single. Always in such eager anticipation to be in a relationship or get married, I disregarded the importance of being by myself. I think as a society we focus so much on "having somebody" that we miss the splendor of being single. As a woman who has been single for roughly 15 months, it wasn't until 4 months ago that I started to see the beauty of singleness.

It was at this point during my self-discovery that I learned as a single woman I have to be careful not to gain an appreciation for being single from a worlds perspective, believing that this season in my life means: "well at least I don't have anyone to worry about" or "I can do what I want to do now that I am single", etc. All these justifications are void fillers that leave us just as empty as we have always been; coddling us with the mindset that promotes failure for yet another relationship. Tell me this, how can one expect to smoothly transition from a selfish phase in their life when they've never practiced healthy benevolence? People lead with this expectation in new relationships all the time and struggle greatly. Your greatest gift to any relationship is knowing who you are and being willing to make adjustment when necessary.

This gift counters much of the madness often associated with being in a relationship or marriage. However, as single women we get so caught up in dating our own way that we totally ignore this gift that aids in healthy relationships. Knowing who you are allows you to recognize the drama and confusion that comes from unhealthy relationships and even helps you recognize unhealthy and broken people.

~How's it Going so Far~

We've discussed a lot of content thus far and I want to make sure you're ok. I know this information can be overwhelming but take heart; it is my goal to introduce to you several areas to address. Some may apply to you and others won't. All in all, the information shared in this book is intended to correct, challenge, ignite change and encourage healthy conversation as you complete your self-discovery as a single woman...and all of this takes TIME! Please understand that before a finished product is exposed to the masses or is ready for purchase it has to go through a ton of processing and development. That process and development is the work you're completing right now on your self-discovery. Trials and tests will come to make sure that the product is proficient enough to withstand its exposure. While you are single it is perfectly normal to experience many trials as well as tests which will ultimately reveal internal issues that could be hindering your effectiveness. When a product fails a test, or proves not sufficient enough to hold up during the trial process, it is sent back to the manufacturer for more work. The same applies in your personal life. During this process, not only are you receiving information you will also be getting many tests.

If I'm 100% honest with you, you won't pass them all the first time around. But be encouraged, if you don't hold up during a trial process you'll be sent back to the manufacturer (Our Creator) for more preparation. As you continue to grow you will understand the importance of asking God to help you complete the work so that you can become better. By asking Him to simply fix the situation you deny yourself vital life experiences that are necessary for your growth. It also suggests a degree of satisfaction with where you are, and opts you out of the learning process. When you opt out of the learning process, you're sure to repeat the same mistake again. With that mindset do you think you are ready for a relationship? Single ladies (and it will continue when you become married ladies) the learning process allows you to appreciate life and equip you to be better not only for yourself but for other women who will battle similar issues you have overcome.

In addition, I also want to make sure that you're prepared to embark upon additional levels of mastery after the learning process is complete. It's equally important to understand that the learning process never ends. It actually gets more in depth as you go through life and encounter various instances of change, differences, new experiences, and people. Take heart, we all go through tests, trials, and processes to make us better, and everything gets better with time.

10

Those Single Mistakes

& Oh There Are Many

L et's move on to common areas we make mistakes in as single women. This also includes women who are dating as well. In this chapter we will explore the areas in our lives that are often misjudged. We will address ways we may be operating in, that don't serve us. This section will provide insight on how we can best navigate certain areas of our lives.

Relationships

Can you agree with me that the number one goal for most singles is to get into a relationship?

It amazes me how for years I desired to be in a relationship so bad that I totally overlooked the vital most important relationships I had. I want to start off with the most important relationship we can ever experience and that is our relationship with God and/or our spiritual relationship. Many people single and/or married do not have this relationship in tact therefore every other relationship they have, or have been in, failed! God is the lover our souls. This means He is our first love. Before we were created in our mother's womb he loved us Jeremiah 1:5. He loved us enough to select that one egg, to connect with our father's sperm to create us. Now that's love. While He chose to love us first we often do not recognize his love until about the 5th 6th or 20th failed attempt at finding love on our own. Some die never getting the chance. The Creators love is free and it's interwoven in our DNA. It does not require anything from us but to accept Him. Yet we opt to buy weave, clothes, cars, and a plethora of other material things and give our bodies away to men all in hopes that they will love us back or show us love when there is love readily available for us without restrictions. One of the mistakes we make as singles is trying to cultivate relationships with everyone but our Creator, our God. Establishing and building our relationship with Him allows us to know and understand the type of love we deserve and equips us to receive the type of relationship He has designed for us.

Look at this example of free love between The Creator and a girl named Beautiful: "Here you go Beautiful; this is a free gift of unconditional love I've tailored just for you"? Beautiful responds, "What do I have to do to get it"? "Absolutely nothing just take it and accept this love in your life" the Creator replies! "This sounds too good to be true, I'm not sure about your offer. I think I'll keep doing things the way I'm accustomed to. Thanks" Beautiful answers and walks away. See how Beautiful declined the gift from the giver and chose to pursue her own quest of finding love? How many times have you seen yourself in Beautiful? Answer the following questions about yourself as a part of the "work" process on your journey.

1. Do you notice any resemblance of yourself in Beautiful? _____

_____

_____

2. You may not have verbally told God "no I don't want your love", but what about your actions? Do you find yourself more concerned about getting into a relationship than seeking God's love for you? If, so why?

_____

_____

_____

_____

3. Are you struggling with letting go of a bad relationship because you are fearful of being alone? If so, what are you afraid of losing? If not, which character traits do you possess that allows you to detach from or avoid bad relationships?_____

_____

_____

_____

_____

_____

4. Do you often find yourself filling up your free time with mindless activities? Such as watching TV, shopping, etc.? If so, what changes can you make to be more intentional about your free time? If not, how do you occupy your free time?

_____

_____

_____

_____

5. How often do you spend time developing your spiritual life? _____

_____

_____

_____

_____

6. Do you find spending time with God difficult or boring? If so, research/follow young influential leaders on social media and/or small groups in your area to join and cultivate that

relationship. List some pages and sites to follow below.

a. _____

b. _____

c. _____

d. _____

e. _____

7. Rank, in the order of importance, each relationship in your life. Start with your most important relationship & what they add to your life? For example: a. Mom- My Rock, b. Cousin Lisa- Always there, c. Billy (Boyfriend)- Consistent, d. God- Hope etc.

a. _____

b. _____

c. _____

a. _____

b. _____

c. _____

d. _____

e. _____

f. _____

g. _____

h. _____

i. _____

The Family

Let's do a heart check! What influenced your ideas about love? Many of us have received our advice about love from the couples in our family. Which is awesome if the couples in your life are wise and bear good fruit? On the contrary if the couples in your life bear bad fruit, (they fight a lot, curse each other out, are self-centered, immature, abusive, etc.) then getting relationship advice from them does not set the foundation for good fruit in your relationships. Do not get me wrong, parents and family members are to be examples of love for us, but Christ represents the greatest example of love for us all. Even if you don't believe in Christ as your spirit leader, His character as a person is a good example to emulate. Prayerfully our parents, grandparents, the married couples in our family, and lastly ourselves refer to Christ's example as our guiding light, showing us how to demonstrate perfect love toward others.

I have talked to countless married couples about every topic imaginable as it relates to marriage and from them I have learned a lot of what to do and what not to do. I have had the pleasure of receiving interesting information from newlywed couples and wisdom from couples married 40 plus years; all sharing their highs, lows, best advice, and things to avoid during relationships and marriage. While some of them offered some really good advice, few of them shared examples that demonstrate Christ's love towards us.

From these various conversations I have learned that every couple shares their love differently and as a result they inadvertently or intentionally give love advice to others as a result of their experiences. Many couples I have spoken with were oblivious to the effect that their relationship had on others, clueless that others were watching and were heavily impacted by what they displayed in their relationship. The manner in which couples relate to each other is one of the most interesting things I have discovered. The complexity of couples' communication and their ability to relate to one another can be astonishing. Please keep in mind as you gather advice from family members, relationship guidance from wise couples provides life giving antidotes. Contrarily, getting advice from other couples may serve as a distraction. For example, I know women who covet others' relationships knowing the relationship is hella dysfunctional. What a distraction! Longing or being envious of something you know isn't bearing any fruit is not beneficial for you.

The ranging degrees of advice I've gained from couples have been scattered abroad. I have met many people that say it's best to hide the truth from their spouse and family especially when children are involved. Now, as a single woman I'd be a fool to take that nugget of information at face values simply because a married family member told me that. It's my responsibility as a single woman to filter information for myself, through my life source, and apply what works for me, discarding the rest. Let's be clear, some information does not need to be broadcasted for the entire world. As stated earlier it's up to you to use discretion as to what information needs to be shared or not. However, many families have been destroyed as a result of this same mindset. Have you seen this attitude or belief reflected in the relationships of those in your life? Do you think this is a good way to show others how to love? I do not care which way you skin a cat, the decision to hide impactful truths teaches others dishonesty. Truth has a distinct way of rising to the surface, whether we want it to or not. The lasting lesson everyone learns as a result of hiding the truth is the consequences of deceitfulness. No, I am not suggesting that you overshare all your business upon meeting someone. There are levels to this, but the extent of vulnerability you and your partner are willing to share be each other, aids in the health factor of your relationship. Relationships have proven to be healthier the more partners are willing to be vulnerable with one another. As singles, we often take a variety of lessons learned from couples around us and attempt to apply them in our dating relationships.

Consequently, applying the wrong advice mixed with our underlying issues, (harbored internally because of our own beliefs) causes us to unintentionally take this negative combination into future relationships. These decisions destroy the people we date, ourselves, and everyone else we're connected to sending us into this repetitive cycle of failed relationships.

On the contrary, a second piece of advice I've gathered from many married couples, is the tendency to keep it too real. This is a huge mistake to apply in your relationships. These couples are likely to argue and fuss unapologetically because they're "so real". Yes, couples like this are real... _misguided_. No one shows love by arguing, fussing or fighting. Doing so translates to others that arguing, fussing, and fighting is the way to express love. Wrong message!

Disagreements happen and are to be expected. The reality is that anytime you put more than one person together, they are bound to disagree at some point. Still, resorting to arguing, fussing and fighting is not the way to resolve issues. Since many single people have witnessed this failed communication regimen from the married people around them, they carry these poor communication qualities into dating relationships. This creates a great deal of internal damage for them and causes significant external and internal damage to their partner or spouse. By understanding the necessity of maximizing our singleness we work on our communication prior to jumping into relationships or pursuing marriage. This results in a greater likelihood of having more meaningful and lasting interactions in our lives. These interactions, be it at work, with family, or strangers, help to prepare us as single women who one day desire a healthy relationship and marriage. Conversely, unless determined to maximize your singleness, you are bound to make the same mistakes continuously in dating relationships. You also begin to adopt those negative traits displayed by those closest to you as well as their characteristics into your relationship/marriage. This provides an unfair disadvantage as it relates to the longevity of your relationships.

The Church

Honestly speaking the advice received from church can be confusing for a single person. It appears that the message "sex before marriage is bad" is the only message being taught to the single men and women in the congregation. Great message, for many reasons but the scare tactic that is subliminally hidden under the message is not of God. The fact that there is more to being single than not having sex seems to be the forgotten message. Typically, the person giving the most advice at church to singles has been married for some time so they only have faint memories of this season. Some of the other people are the young newlywed couples, so happy they are no longer single that somehow, I guess as a side effect of bliss, they forgot the struggles of singleness. It is often preached that all of your free time should be of service to the Lord. This is a noble concept but let's be real... every bit of your free time? Really?! If you take that message for face value you will be confused and furthermore turned off from the single life. Some Singles Ministries are structured in such a way that the attendees are not supposed to date the other single members in the church. Another perplexing message. It puzzles me because if you preach that the world is supposed to be the big, bad place and the church supposedly our safe haven, why on earth would you not want the singles in the church to meet and greet? There may truly be a love match there.

Personally, I view it as a means of dictatorship but there could be pure motives that I have not been privy to witnessing. Please keep in mind this observation is not of every church but of my personal experience, which is also similar to the experiences of a few in my immediate circle.

To bring about clarity, yes there is an advantage in your singleness to spend valuable time with Christ uninterrupted but that does not mean you cannot or should not enjoy all that life has to offer. One noted difference between religious people and non-religious people is that people of the world know how to enjoy life, while religious people are so busy making rules and worrying about who's keeping them or not that they have a tendency to miss all the fun. Look at Ecclesiastes 8:15. Singles ministry is a great outlet to explore growth in your singleness but if not lead properly I see how it can be a turn off. Explore the content and structure of the singles ministry at your church before you join, exercising discernment. Although you may be single, your pastor may not agree with me, the singles ministry at your church may not be the ministry most suitable for you. I encourage all people, but for the sake of this book, singles, to utilize discernment as it relates to how you should conduct your life. I also want to add, it is not good for man to be alone. God knew that the day He created man. He gave Adam purpose

Those Single Mistakes

then a woman, and the two became one. Through sin, corruption, and our own selfishness we have begged God to let us have our way and that is exactly what we got as a result...prolonged singleness; because of our determination. If you're honest with yourself, where has that gotten us? We can't blame ole Eve anymore, her husband, (also known as her earthly leader), the snake or anyone else for what's going on today. Honestly, our personal actions further prove that if we were put in the same situation we would have done the same thing. If you don't think so ask yourself, how hard is it for me to obey God now? I'm just being honest.

The Media

In addition to gaining knowledge from the couples around us on how to love and the church, we also have the media, which plays a huge role in how we relate to others. We have reality TV which has taken over the air waves and invaded our dwelling places. It portrays men lavishing their wives, girlfriends, or fiancés with gifts or the ability to gain publicity and women fighting and demoralizing themselves for

154

attention. It's easy to be blinded by the glitz and glamour, so much so that we fail to realize the reality. These same guys witnessed on our flat screens struggle with difficulties that if we're honest with ourselves, we don't want those issues. For instance, staying out of prison or the drug game; Or his uncontrollable desire to express his anger or passion so he fights a lot or can't stay out of other women's beds. Yet somehow, we conveniently gloss over those facts. Reality TV encourages its viewers to define a person's character by what they display on the exterior and the amount of material-ism they have attained. We quickly turn a blind eye to the details beyond their televised relationships, caring not to question what's really going on and summing it all up as: "Well at least he takes care of home". I have even been in conversations with women who have said "I don't mind having a man who disrespects me or makes illegal money as long as I'm taken care of, after all he is a man. What more do you expect"? The sad part is these conversations are happening more frequently the further we glamorize these negative depictions of men and relationships.

It's numbing the impact singleness can have on single women when you see beautiful queens becoming robotized to the customs and beliefs of this world. Women are beginning to believe the lies of what a man is and how he is to treat them; while allowing the enemy's influence to have a greater impact in their lives as opposed to the influence of God. We find it difficult to believe any man exists who has not developed the world's mindset or who is able to outgrow it, hence the likelihood of settling for the first thing smoking in hopes that he may be the one. Well I will tell you, there are men who abhor the values of this world and are looking for real women who understand their value, are confident in Christ, and understand their role as a man, and in society. Furthermore, with the power of God any man, woman, boy or girl can become who He's called them to be. The enemy would have you to believe the opposite in hopes of keeping you in bondage, deterring you from maximizing your singleness, and setting you up for yet another botched relationship. Don't buy into it! I will also tell you that a real man does not harbor the beliefs and glorified customs of this world. The unfaithful men previously discussed who have been validated by society, have the genetic makeup of a man but is unwilling to handle the God given responsibility attached to manhood. Is that the type of man you want to be committed to? At best these kinds of men are unenlightened species with a penis, a skewed brain, and an extremely damaged heart. Not the type of man God has for you and not the type of man you should desire. I dare not compare the Man above, who is to be the example for all of us, to that kind of unenlightened individual: no way no how, just won't do it!

Now is a grown man capable of making mistakes, you better know it! Men can, just as you can, mess up, do things they aren't proud of and so forth. That's a part of the human experience. However, it's necessary to keep in mind before you start making excuses for blatant disrespect or excusing willful behavior, anyone is capable of change but only with divine direction, not yours. In addition, one thing that speaks volumes of a persons' character is their ability to own their faults and teach others that their negative actions are not the way to a fulfilled life. This kind of message is rarely displayed on reality TV. These men also admit their mistakes and work diligently not to make them again, another characteristic rarely shown on TV.

If you believe the notion that reality TV does not affect you, think again. What goes into your eyes, ears, mouth, and body affects you. If you don't believe me go on a reality TV fast and monitor your attitude in general. There will be a noticeable difference.

Educating the Singles

Back to the Basics

After the fruitless endeavor of attempting to mirror our family, friends, church, and the media's relationship advice, we should be directed to pursue the primary source, a stable place to receive relationship guidance from, God. As a single woman our greatest assets is to develop our spiritual relationship. Many of us have been so occupied with dysfunctional relationships that we're unable to understand that those same dysfunctional tendencies are hindering us from receiving the intended benefit of our spiritual life. Our Creator is functioning and through our dysfunction we experience a strain on our relationships with Him. Because our Creator cannot be moved, He's unbothered by our dysfunction, consequently it's we who suffer and create distance between ourselves and God. Dysfunctional relationships are designed by the enemy, who offers confusion as a means to establish a distorted perception of love, relationships, and the value of singleness. If you're involved in or are accustomed to dysfunction in your relationships, expose the enemies' tactics and call him out. Declare that you will no longer subject yourself to malfunctioning relationships but only to positive and beneficial dealings with others. Glean from spiritual truths using that guidance to show you how to love and be loved. Our Creator of all Truth is available at your request. As you seek Him for guidance on how to love yourself and others, you will find His revelation to be your greatest resource as a single woman.

Luke 11: 10

"For everyone who asks, receives. Everyone who seeks, finds. And to

everyone who knocks, the door will be opened".

Next, I am going to share tools you can use to help you further develop your spiritual relationship. It is imperative that the health of our spiritual relationship is operating at an optimal level, so we can identify and forge relationships with people who are capable of watering us. In order to develop a healthy spiritual relationship, we have to spend time in the spirit. Spending time with The Creator is not limited to you constantly unloading and never refueling. Talking repetitively about your problems, your wants, and your desires, never allowing Truth to speak back, you usually feel empty after all that unloading with nothing to fill you back up. If you're honest, there's a possibility that you've seen similar patterns in your previous relationships. If so, this more than likely resulted in you being the person in the relationship always having something to say but never listening or always giving but getting nothing in return. Many people have a one-sided spiritual relationship because they are unaware that the Spirit desires to speak back. How do you know when God is speaking? There are a few sure signs that help you determine if it's God speaking or if it's the enemy.

#1 When God speaks it is often going to be the opposite of what our flesh wants or desires. He regularly speaks and tells us things that we are not ready to accept or willing to hear. While it may seem discouraging at the moment, the lasting result of following our Spirt is sure to bring about greater results than we could ever imagine.

#2 What God says can be backed in scripture. God may not speak a direct Bible passage to you that you can research and find in the Bible verbatim; but the underlying content of its principles can be found in scripture.

#3 That voice on the inside of us which many people refer to as a woman's intuition is in fact God's voice. His voice has the capacity to speak loudly, resounding throughout your entire body. This power affects your very core, resorting in a feeling of uneasiness that transpires when you are contemplating a potentially hazardous decision. Additionally, it cautions you as it relates to the ill intentions of others. We often hear this voice but choose to ignore it. We often hear God speaking but because the issue is something we do not wish to address, we ignore Him. God also speaks through people, circumstance and consequences as well.

Has this happened in your personal life? Maybe a family member, friend, or ex wanted to tell you something about yourself that you did not want to hear? What were they trying to tell you? Was there any validity to it? If not, this next part doesn't apply to that person or that relationship but could serve some benefit in the future. However, if you have experienced this after a failed relationship now is the most opportune time to ask yourself, "Was my ex right"? Maybe not 100% right, but was there some truth to anything said about me in the relationship? Careful to catch you before you get too lost down memory lane. If you do agree that an ex had some validity concerning you, your attitude, personality, behaviors, etc. this does not mean that your breakup was a huge mistake. While your flaws may have carried much weight in the demise of that relationship, please keep in mind the door on that relationship has been closed. There is more you need to process before running back to a situation that was left damaged. So, if the above proves true, your ex was right, this revelation does not suggest that you call your ex tonight and let him know he is the one for you or that you made a huge mistake and desire reconciliation.

No matter your contribution to the ending of the relationship, there are always other factors that subsidize. Simply put, you know if the relationship was garbage in the first place. As we all know it's easy after breakups to get amnesia; especially after time has lapsed. It's also easy to experience loneliness as well which often causes us to overlook all the drama and disrespect endured in that same relationship (if applicable). Remember, breakups happen for a reason and it's often bigger than what you did or what he did or did not do. Pray and ask God to lead you as it relates to digging up issues from the past. Also don't be afraid to seek professional assistance as well. Counseling or coaching in addition to prayer is often necessary.

I also want to share a valuable secret with you; in order to effectively hear Him speak, it takes time. There is no way to get an accurate understanding of what God is saying if you have not spent any time with Him in prayer, reading, and/or meditation. Admitting that an ex, or person in your life was right, is the first step to moving in the right direction. I encourage you to examine your past relationships and explore your involvement in them. Good or bad, each experience is designed to teach us new lessons and there is something for you to learn about you, even after a bad or messy breakup.

God sometimes uses undesirable circumstances and unqualified individuals as vessels to share His wisdom with us. This revelation of wisdom is designed to turn our focus to Him not on our past circumstances, relationships, or friendships. So let the past serve as a learning tool, not a repeat lesson. You can explore the past to gain more knowledge without picking it up and repeating the same thing over and over again. The ability to do this requires discipline and clear direction on where you're going and what you're trying to gain. As you embark on this part of the process, take time to explore your willingness and ability to hear the voice of the Lord. As you explore your past, He will show you areas in which you could have made different decisions, chose better methods, listened more, spoke less, etc. Sometimes God requires a separation between two people just to bring you to this place, back to Him desperate for answers and change. If we're not careful our emotions or loneliness will have us to believe that God wants us to move backwards with the person instead of forward with Him. This distinction can best be made as your relationship with God develops. This gives you the ability to decipher the difference between God's voice and the enemy's voice in your life. Knowing the distinction is vital because the enemy used to be an angel in heaven, so he knows the things of God and is well versed in scripture. Sometimes things of God can be convoluted with the enemy if you aren't aware.

The next thing you can do as a single woman to develop your spiritual life is to learn more about it. How can you learn more about God? We briefly talked about it earlier. The most effective way to develop your spiritual relationship is by implementing the trio: reading, studying, and meditating on His words. The life of Jesus demonstrates selfless acts such as offering His life as a guiding blueprint to show us how we are to conduct our lives. Throughout his ministry Jesus teaches us how to endure hard times and persecution, the importance of helping and blessing others, the necessity of depending on God through both good times and bad, how to enjoy life and have fun, and lastly how to establish and build healthy relationships. Do not limit Jesus to the box of religious interpretation; get to know Truth for yourself. There are numerous instances where Jesus went out and had fun. He partied and enjoyed all types of people, yet they did not influence Him, He influenced them. To be the influencer in your relationships you must study the blueprint and follow its instructions as you build your relationships and continue to model your lifestyle accordingly. Here are just a few examples on how Jesus had fun in case you didn't believe me!

Matthew 11:19

[19] *"The Son of man came eating and drinking, and they say, Behold a man gluttonous, and a winebibber, a friend of publicans and sinners. But wisdom is justified of her children".*

John 2: 1-12

"The next day[a] there was a wedding celebration in the village of Cana in Galilee. Jesus' mother was there, [2] and Jesus and his disciples were also

invited to the celebration. ³ The wine supply ran out during the festivities, so Jesus' mother told him, "They have no more wine".

Mark 2:14-16

⁴ *"As he walked along, he saw Levi son of Alphaeus sitting at his tax collector's booth. "Follow me and be my disciple," Jesus said to him. So Levi got up and followed him.¹⁵ Later, Levi invited Jesus and his disciples to his home as dinner guests, along with many tax collectors and other disreputable sinners. (There were many people of this kind among Jesus' followers.) ¹⁶ But when the teachers of religious law who were Pharisees[b] saw him eating with tax collectors and other sinners, they asked his disciples, "Why does he eat with such scum"?[c]"*

What is the status of your relationship with God: active, inactive, or nonexistent? Take time to fully develop this relationship every single day. This relationship serves as the guiding light to lead your character and help you nurture healthy connections with others.

1. How frequently do you study about God and His principles and or develop your spiritual life? _____

_____

_____

_____

2. How consistent is your prayer life or communication with God and how can you further develop it?

_____

_____

_____

_____

3. Do you believe you can hear God speak? If so, how does He communicate with you?

_____

_____

_____

_____

4. Do you consider your conversations with God to be one sided or mutually equitable & how?

_____

_____

_____

_____

_____

_____

_____

_____

_____

There is no set amount of time to spend developing your spiritual life. One thing I love about our Creator is that He isn't controlling. He gives us free will to do whatever we want. The good thing about that is He isn't ready to punish us if we don't read the Bible, talk to Him, or go to church! All of that is beneficial to us. I liken it to working out. We all know working out is good for us and the more we workout the more in shape we become. If we choose not to work out and be out of shape the only lives we're affecting is ours. If our health fails as a result of our negligence, we will begin to affect the lives of those closest to us. Equally, even if we committed to working out just a little, we would be in better shape than we would be if we didn't work out at all. Furthermore, can you imagine the results you'd see if you worked out several times a week? To fulfill the goal for an optimal life, we should be fully in shape physically, mentally, and spiritually. In order to be in shape spiritually we must exercise our faith muscles, read the Word, pray, and have conversations with God.

Relationships 101

Since we have talked about the best way to establish and build the most influential relationship you will ever have, your spiritual relationship, we will now discuss another relationship to be working on and developing as a single woman. This is the relationship with your family. Some of you, like I, grew up in an extremely family oriented environment. Raised to love your family above all else. You may spend as much time as you can with your loved ones, year after year anticipating the holiday season because that appears to be the only time everyone can truly get together. More than likely it's habitual for you to speak with an aunt, uncle, parent, sibling, grandparent or cousin at some point during the week, and it's quite likely that you even mention their names during prayers before bed. However, even with my strong family roots I have been guilty of haphazardly developing relationships with some of my family members. I will talk in more depth about that later but I want to address the direct opposite of those family oriented individuals just discussed. These are the people who can't stand their family or at least some of its members. For some this is a result of unimaginable situations that have happened in the family or decisions that defy their approval. Many women carry grudges against members in their family for things that happened years ago, some big and some small. Before we get too carried away here, let's set this disclaimer, in some cases there are healthy boundaries that need to be established between yourself and certain members in your family. Love does not always show up through the act of rescuing someone or bridging the distance between you. For some, the only way to effectively display love is to create healthy space. That is what Christ did after He died and went on to be with God. He created some distance between Him and us so that we could *learn* to draw closer to Him. Giving us the opportunity to realize that He is ever present, dependable and the missing link sought after in our lives. Some live life and still miss the opportunity, but the distance was still necessary. I also don't want to neglect those who are estranged from family due to tragedy or other life instances. My deepest sympathy goes out to you. Nevertheless, there are other relationships that can be established to help you move past your loss and become better prepared for romantic relationships. All is not lost.

Ok, so back to women who are experiencing difficulty building or maintaining a family relationship. I am totally aware of the seriousness associated with major family issues as it relates to neglect, abuse, or legal issues that are beyond a person's control. However, I want to talk about women who have separated themselves from family members as a result of petty offenses. Those situations that involve money, past neglect from a family member (who has since been trying to rectify the issue for years, but your hard heart rejects every attempt) an argument, disproval of a past relationship that you (or they) are no longer involved in, and so forth. Now is the time to let that go. I hate to be the one to tell you but people are going to hurt you in this life. Physical hurt, however in any relationship is unhealthy. Intentional verbal and emotional hurt are equally as morbid and should not be tolerated. Just as you and I have hurt others by our words, attitude, and non-volatile actions; others will hurt us in the same ways. If you think getting into a relationship with someone is going to eliminate the propensity of you experiencing hurt feelings, baby girl you, are in for a rude awaking. Just as sure as I am alive and breathing your one-day spouse is going to hurt your feelings at least once. Furthermore, a real truth is that in some cases our feelings may need to be hurt a time or two to help put some things into perspective. Let's be clear, if someone is in your life that is demeaning, degrading, fighting and/or abusing you, or bringing about any form of intentional hurt that person is not for you. That is a relationship that does not reflect love and needs to be severed. But sometimes ladies when we do not get our way, a well-placed hurt feeling may be vital for our growth. Sometimes our feelings are hurt not as a result of something offensive but as a defensive mechanism to protect a hardened heart or excuse our questionable actions. This may be a good time to stop reading and do a heart check as it relates to motives, manipulation, and feelings.

1. If applicable, why do you want to be in a romantic relationship? _____

_____

_____

_____

_____

2. Have you or are you willing to share the reasons listed above to your future or current partner?_____

_____

_____

3. What are some known benefits you've personally received from your previous romantic relationship? What benefits do you desire to receive from your future relationship?

PAST:_____

_____

_____

_____

FUTURE:_____

_____

_____

_____

4. Have you ever been manipulated in a past relationship? If so, what signs will you look out for to avoid a repeat of this in your future relationship? _____

_____

_____

_____

_____

5. Have you ever manipulated someone or have been manipulative in a past/current relationship? If, so how; and what areas in your personal life do you need to develop to avoid manipulation in your future or current relationship? _____

_____

_____

_____

_____

_____

One of God's purposes for family is the opportunity to share and practice our love with others. Due to our familiarity and casualness, it's easy to devalue that wonderful opportunity. Some women can't find one justifiable reason why they are estranged from family members. Some hate their mothers for accepting their fathers or stepfathers' infidelity, some hold disdain towards their fathers for being at work all the time, or choosing to be absent, and a variety of other issues that are too vast to name. While a family member may be totally wrong, and to this day still insists on validating their wrongness, it benefits us to realize that people are people and everyone lives and operates in a way that makes sense to them at that time. Some choose denial and living in denial makes all the sense in the world to them; however, you do not have to adopt their negative ways of doing things. I am not suggesting that you become overly engaged with them but forgiveness is necessary.

Philippians 3: 13-14

¹³" No, Christian brothers, I do not have that life yet. But I do one thing. I forget everything that is behind me and look forward to that which is ahead of me. ¹⁴ My eyes are on the crown. I want to win the race and get the crown of God's call from heaven through Christ Jesus".

Also remember this; it's impossible to fully forgive without letting go of the painful memory. You may never forget but you must release it. It's like you desiring an orange but you have an apple in both of your hands. You know the apple is in your hand, right? You've held those apples for weeks, but now it's time for you to let one of those apples go. In order to get the orange, you desire you have to place the apple in someone else's hand. Remember, no one can change a person other than God, no matter how hard you try, you cannot accomplish it. It's not until you let go of the apple that you will receive the orange. Will you forget about the apple? Maybe, maybe not, but to get what you desire you must let it go. Forgiveness is real and an issue that needs to be handled prior to entering any relationship and especially romantic ones. It's unhealthy to begin a relationship with someone while still holding onto past hurts. It's also dangerous to be in a relationship refusing to forgive or continue a relationship if you're afraid to offer love because of previous failures in your romantic, platonic, or family affairs.

In addition, be mindful of how you show love. Many women display a phony love, concealing unforgiveness and hurt deep within. They often present to the world an idealized imagery of someone totally opposite from the woman they truly are. This phony love manipulates others because they are unaware of who they really are, until life circumstances occur that unveils their truth. Be aware that trying to fool others and even attempting to fool yourself is possible but only you and God truly know the real secrets of your heart. I am also of the opinion, that some women who excessively boast or brag about the love they have for their family or loved ones may be doing so in an attempt to make others think they have the capacity to love at a level they have yet to develop. On the contrary, you don't want to be the woman sharing all the negative feelings you have towards the people in your family either. I call this information overload; sharing with others too much information as it relates to how you interact with your family! With maturity, you gain a sense of balance and instead of harboring that unforgiveness and disdain towards a certain family member; opting to work on forgiveness and love within, helps you become authentic in what you say and do. All of this is vital self-discovery prior to entering any relationship. Once in a relationship your partner doesn't need your instability. Saying you feel one way about him or the relationship, but truly feeling another, sets the relationship up for failure. Women who only feel safe by displaying phony love often do this. They are often oblivious to the unnecessary drama and tension that develops in the relationship, the time wasted, and ultimately the perception they give of being conflicted. As a single woman you want to get into the habit of actively pursuing being the best YOU daily and practicing honesty with yourself and others. Unforgiveness of the past, especially wrongs suffered due to family, destroys you from the inside out and sets your future relationship up for a lose/lose situation. Additionally, carrying preconceived notions, hurt feelings, anticipated failures, and warped views of marriage from past family disappointments into a potentially long-term relationship, hinders any room for authentic love to grow and develop in your life.

What about your friends? Friends are often chosen for the wrong reasons. As women, we choose friends based on a variety of factors. Some friends are chosen because of their appearance, popularity, wit, or their keep it real personality. Friends are also chosen based upon similarities such as children playing for the same team, attending the same church or working at the same office. Sometimes friendships are chosen based on deficits or dysfunction such as suffering bitter divorces, extreme cases of loneliness or brokenness even instances where one satisfies the others desire to feel needed. Other times, friends are chosen based on what they can do for the other. For example, social perks like getting someone into VIP or the notoriety they have acclaimed because they date ballers or are well connected; they may even be a baller themselves. All in all, we select individuals as friends for one reason or another and no matter our reason each friend plays a major role in our lives. Conversely, friendships should be mutual in which you are equally serving a purpose in each other's lives.

Selecting friends based on surface gains, prioritizing only what they can do for us or befriending them based on external or materialistic qualities, will ensure that you won't have a friend left in the end.

Remember as you continue to move forward the motives discussed that serve as a great foundation for amazing friendships. Right now, we are going to assess your friendships. Ask yourself the following questions:

1.What is my definition of a friend?_____

_____

_____

_____

_____

2. What does it take for me to call someone my friend, or even my best friend?

_____

_____

_____

_____

_____

_____

3. Based upon your requirements of friendship, do you offer the friends in your life the same benefits?

_____

_____

_____

_____

_____

4. Who is your closest friend and why?

_____

_____

_____

_____

5. What do you think is the recipe for a lasting or healthy friendship and do you classify your friendships as healthy?

_____

_____

_____

_____

Perfect! Next, I am going to ask you a series of questions that you don't necessarily have to write down, however, these questions serve as food for thought. Do any of you and your friends share a similar moral or value system? It's unrealistic to think you will see eye to eye with friends on all issues but even after disagreements, for the most part, are your girlfriends supportive of you. Do they encourage you, and do they challenge you to be better? If you do not have anyone around you with those characteristics my friend it's time to assess your friendships! Now, you may be wondering how does my friendships relate to my singleness? In several ways! On my journey to self-discovery, I learned that I needed to do a friend check to determine the type of people I allowed in my space. It became apparent to me that before any romantic relationship can be established, a friendship should be built first. This caused me to truly take an assessment of the friendships I had in my life.

If your current friends are trifling then how easy it is for you to develop friendships with trifling men who you'd hope to one day build a relationship with? I remember during this part of the process I wanted to hold on to some lifeless friendships and it was at that moment I had to be real with myself. I had to face the facts that it's easy to make excuses for people all day long if that made me feel better. Yet, at the end of it all, operating in denial and refusal to accept the facts about the people in my life would leave me feeling alone, underappreciated and frustrated, ultimately lacking healthy friendships and relationships. So I did what needed to be done. I kept that which was good and discarded the rest and the same truth applies to you. If it's lifeless why are you holding onto it?

Another characteristic of a friend is one that is supportive of you. Do your friends pray for you and with you? If not, why? Do you pray for and with your friends? Why or why not? If you pay close attention, the friends that don't believe in the power of prayer are often the neediest because they search for solutions in individuals instead of their higher power. These friends will often come to you with their problems and issues and seemingly leave them on your doorstep. It's like they come to you, unload, then walk away feeling free and leaving you with their mess. These friends slowly suck the life out of you, adding *their* baggage to your personal pile of struggles you're already filtering through. They have the tendency to take advantage of or hone in on your loneliness and stifle your progress. How? Because they aren't reciprocative friends. Friends that reciprocate understand the power of giving and receiving and when they have nothing left to give they understand the power of prayer. Prayer breeds life. Given your everyday hustle and bustle as well as the energy you put into your friendships (going out, talking on the phone, listening to their drama, etc.) the very least they can do is replenish you with prayer, positive energy, or encouragement. That's the role of a friend!

Now, the question surfaces as a believer can you have unsaved friends? Yes. I love dearly a few women who are unsaved. Remember everyone who claims salvations is not saved so you can't limit the unsaved friends to the ones who cuss like a sailor, drink until there is no memory left, or has a plethora of men rotating in and out of their bed. An unsaved friend can faithfully sit her cute self on a pew in a church house every weekend and still be as unsaved as they can be. So yes, you can have unsaved friends. However, there is a level of spiritual maturity that is necessary to continue those friendships. Have I always had the level of spiritual maturity needed to maintain friendships with unsaved women? No. That's why they had as much influence over my life as they did during our friendship. Why is spiritual maturity necessary when participating in a friendship with an unbeliever? Spiritual maturity helps you create healthy boundaries in these friendships. It also helps you say no, when necessary. For example, at some points in your life God may be telling you to take a break from going out but you have some unsaved friends who always want to hang out at the club. When this group of girls ask you if you would like to join them, as they paint the town red? If you already know God has told you to take a break, you will be strong enough to decline the invitation, as opposed to giving that reluctant "well I guess I'll go". We are all familiar with that "well I guess I'll go" which translates to you going out anyway and having a horrible experience.

Am I saying that a person who goes to the club is unsaved? No! I do believe that if you are of age going out with friends is totally acceptable. Taking everything into account, it's all about motive. If your motives are pure, then by all means, why not live it up. All this to say, by choosing to be clear and confident about your motives, you'll experience the liberty to enjoy your journey and be fully present with your friends.

If a man of substance just so happens to cross your path, he'd be able to recognize the fruit of your work. But Chica, keep in mind the objective should never be to go out and be on the hunt for him. The objective is to enjoy life. There is nothing wrong with liking to be complemented by men or people in general, but it's your motives that need to remain in check. If you are going out to intentionally gain compliments or attention, there is a strong possibility that you are experiencing a void in your life. This void looks like a sense of desperation as you aimlessly begin the quest of attempting to fill your emptiness with sketchy praise. Real friends recognize that and aren't afraid to have a truth moment with you.

Romance 101

One commonality among single women is the mistakes we make in our relationship choices. Really quickly, let's get some groundwork out of the way. For some, there are only two relationship categories: Single or Married. For others there are three: Single, Dating, or Married and lastly a group that identities with four: Single, Dating, in a Relationship/ Courting, or Married. No opinion is right or wrong however if you are unmarried, traditionally you are single. It's nothing to get mad about, it's just tradition. That doesn't negate your relationship if you are in one and it doesn't mean the other variations are inaccurate. It's just the notion that if you're not married, you're technically single. No biggie, please don't over think this.

As we all know all relationships between a guy and a girl do not have the "boyfriend/ girlfriend" title; some are sex buddies, a permanent boo thing, or the hopeful Mr. Mister. The hopeful Mr. Mister is the man you like a whole lot, but he's just not that into you. Come on ladies, you know you have been involved with or know a friend who continually becomes involved with different guys that don't even have the dignity or respect to make them (or you) their girlfriend. For whatever reason, these guys have an issue publicizing the relationship, but privately there seems to be no issues at all. I have been that chick. We will discuss sexual relationships later but, I truly want to hone in on the type of guys we desire and the importance of character. I, like many people, refuse to call these guys men because they have no idea what manhood is. It goes beyond an age requirement and focuses on the level of character that has been developed over the years. I cannot begin to tell you how many guys I wanted to be with so bad who were not even worth a ½ second of my time but because they were fine, had a little bit of notoriety, or a good job I was gung ho on being theirs. I had determined in my mind that was all the fundamental requirements I needed from a guy to establish a meaningful relationship. My thought process was so aloof that I rated potential partners on the characteristics of looks, notoriety, and work ethic. Oh, and how can I forget that golden trait: He had to go to church? What type of garbage had I created in my head for a man? The potential leader of my family needed to look good, work, and go to church. His relationship with God meant nothing to me, if he at least claimed salvation I was certain that my saved self could cultivate him into the God-fearing man he was born to be, according to my understanding. I will never forget the day when God asked me why I wanted that responsibility? The responsibility of cultivating a grown guy into a man and leader. Number one that is extremely insulting to God; me attempting to take God's job away from Him and have the audacity to think that I would be able to do His job better than He, performing a miracle by my own merit. Secondly, that is not the role of a woman. God's intention for women is not to nurture a grown guy into manhood. The original position filler for that job is God himself and that guys parents. If the second party dropped the ball, his parents, it is certainly not God's design for you as a woman to fill the position.

12

Building Singleness: What you Need & Don't Need

Beginning Anew

The necessary formula for a fulfilled single life and a lasting relationship which could lead to a rewarding marriage is self-awareness and a strong foundation. That is the purpose of this book...to help guide you as you build upon a solid foundation. I have been guilty of believing that perhaps a relationship could survive without these fundamentals. I have even gone so far as to verbalize after a few encounters with couples who aren't grounded that these components may not be the necessary ones for a healthy marriage; after all they appeared to be doing just fine without them. Thank God, He will not leave us ignorant; He immediately shut that down and shared with me the importance of foundation. If a building is built on a faulty foundation it is sure to crumble. This crumbling could take place immediately or wait until several decades have passed but the reality is the building will eventually fall. Sometimes from the inside out. In addition, faulty foundations and construction leads to many expensive problems. Can these problems be fixed? Sure, they can but it often costs more than what was bargained for and more often than not, it proves to not be worth it. Compare this to relationships, can a couple push past faulty foundations; Absolutely! However, the couple will struggle immensely to reach their maximal level of achievement and satisfaction. The world we live in rejects wholeness and encourages us to build relationships with broken pieces. We get so caught up in what's going on right now, who's hot right not, and how we feel right now that we attempt to build relationships off emotions and what we think we can gain to ultimately benefit us. Our requirements are belittled to superficial characteristics and our ideal is limited to today's trending topics. We look at the relationships of reality stars, musicians, and athletes and use those relationships as our reference point on how we are to conduct our lives. We make decisions based on external happenings, neglecting the repercussions and impact that those decisions will have on the rest of our lives. We are guilty of building our lives, relationships, and even our mental health with futile materials and faulty blue prints, blinding us to the reality around us.

This tendency tricks us into believe that the portrayed state of our favorite reality couples' relationship on the latest episode, or any other public figure for that matter, saved or unsaved, is the actuality of that relationship. We forget that these random shows are somewhat staged, taped months before airing, and are not to serve as model relationships for us. Like really, we are comparing and lusting for relationships that are staged, outdated, and lasts for 30 minutes at a time! All this to say: as people we can not only be concerned with what we see right now we must assess situations beyond the surface. We can't see the divorce or separation that lies at the end of the relationship we lust after or are envious of. We can't even see what's happening behind closed doors, when the cameras are not rolling.

When we choose not to address the truth behind anything that is going on in or around us, we allow unnecessary room for comparison and envy that wouldn't be so if we paid more attention to the reality, truth, and most importantly our personal truth. We tend to become blinded by the aspects of others' lives and ignore the detrimental elements because we sum it up as "none of our business", and we walk around defeated to the truth of God's Word, and the destruction tied to the enemy's tactics which are designed to throw us off track. I also want to reiterate this for my church goers, just because people are in the church does not mean they are the ones for you and if church isn't your thing; don't buy off into the enemy's influence or promptings that may cause you to say "I know a whole lot of church people getting a divorce, or cheating on their spouse so what's the difference"? Here's the difference, Character! I, like you, know many people who go to church that do a whole lot of crazy things and it has nothing to do with their church attendance but everything to do with their character. The word character is a divine principle that's based on moral qualities. There are individuals from all backgrounds who lack character and the desire to seek those with upstanding character comes from discernment and patience. Without our spiritual life we can do nothing, nothing lasts, nothing is stable, and everything fails. There is no in between.

People make bad decisions about who they marry because they chose not to maximize their singleness, and they totally ignored spiritual guidance during the dating process. The enemy, who is the opposite of Truth, comes to steal, kill, and destroy. He specializes in making everything look great on the outside, all the while destroying it immensely from the inside out. It's rare that we witness many happily married couples today and have you ever wondered why? It is because people are not connected, they haven't done the work and they aren't intentional. As a single woman you can't afford to ignore the voice of God and His guidance. Ladies, you can't get with the first man who pays you some attention, knowing good and well you have not the slightest clue who this man really is. All these emotional decisions lead to relationships that are damaged and marriages that end in divorce. And when people are not committed to doing what is required of them as single men or women, it's extremely difficult for them to do what is required of them in a marriage. It is also the enemy's crooked plan to present these falsely represented relationships and marriages to women so that we covet them in our hearts, and indirectly base our belief system and the way we conduct our relationship on the world's standards. We cannot do things our own way and slap God or spirituality in it and think that somehow, He is involved. He is not. There is a plan created for relationships and it involves a clear process. The process may not be the same for everyone but if we seek Truth and follow the process designed for us, we reap the rewards associated on every level. If we don't follow the process we make the journey more difficult and harder to maneuver on each level.

13

Never Settle

You Don't Need: The At Least

At least, at least at least! Have you ever been caught saying "well at least he", or "at least I", or "at least they"? Aren't you tired of the "at least". Have you ever considered the "MOST"? What is the <u>most</u> he can do, or the <u>most</u> you can do, or the <u>most</u> they can do, or the <u>most</u> that God has for you? Have you ever considered that maybe the least is all you have been given because that's all you expect? Next, we will discuss the three "at least" statements that single women use about men that are extremely limiting and damaging to their potential.

They Go to Church

Ladies saying that all a person must do is go to church, will land you with the devil himself. A person can go to church every time the door opens, camouflage their way into the hearts of women all to revel their ulterior motives of selfishness and deceit. Reflect on your past relationships and point out the little devils you've encountered along the way! You may be able to laugh now but when you were involved it was not a funny matter. Be careful what you ask for in a mate because being so vague as to say, "at least he goes to church" will have you settle for a crazy man who "at least goes to church". Try merging that with a few of those other vain qualities you came up with all wrapped up into a 6-foot-tall fine specimen, hell sent. As a mature woman you begin to understand that God is all knowing. You begin to trust that He has the very best for you. You will understand that while some of your desires may be valid, He has something or someone better for you. You will also experience, as you develop your relationship with Him, a change in your desires. God will identify, rearrange, or even substitute your desires and send you who and what you need, when you need it. Once you understand these things you will begin to see that going to church means nothing. A man can go to church every Sunday and still be a liar, cheater, abuser, and an ill-equipped individual to try and pursue a relationship with.

Do you not trust God enough to give you the desires of your heart governed by what He knows is best for you? Why do we as women struggle with trusting God but we are willing to dive head first into a relationship with someone we know nothing about? As women we cannot afford to get impatient with God and influenced by everything going on around us, that the slightest man who pays us any attention, or who fits our "list" and goes to church, gets our undivided attention. Or be so jaded by our past that we run behind guys who could care less if we were dead or alive and wouldn't even know the difference, but he goes to church so that somehow means he has to be the one for us? "At least he goes to church" is not going to cut it!

They Have Money

While some women are concerned about the church attendance of their partner or even their looks, there are some that could care less about those aspects. The women we'll discuss next are the ones solely concerned about a person's financial status, perceived or actual. They have developed the mentality that if a man communicates with them in some form on a relatively consistent basis or not, knows how to show them a good time and introduces them to "the life" they always wanted, he has their heart, mind, body, and soul. But why?

Who's to say this man does not acquire or profess to acquire large amounts of money to lure anxious women like you? In hopes of using every dollar spent as an investment to one day own you? Women who chase someone based on their financial status rarely take into consideration that these kinds of individuals tend to take ownership of those they support financially. Not all, but a great deal of them do. It's often not realized until the demands required of her are not what she bargained for. Initially, she is blinded by the proclivity he displays to help her look good until he starts demeaning her. Thereby, making her look bad, stupid, or feeling useless. Then she wakes up one day with all the money, all the clothes, shoes and bags but no soul. Are we not more than the external? Ask the fashion, hair, and diet industry. Given their profit margin women sure don't act like it. I once heard a saying if you marry for money you earn every bit of it. Money cannot buy you happiness, we all know that. Money can't make a man respect, love, or value you either. While money may have a face value it's still paper. Building a relationship with paper ensures its demise and increases its flammability.

I Got a Man

Last, but not least, we have the women who don't care much about money, don't care much about looks, Christ or anything else. Their major concern is SIMPLY having a man. They want to have a man for the sole purpose of saying "well at least I got a man". These women are those who feel they need a man regardless if he's married, engaged, in a relationship, or has multiple girlfriends. Women who intentionally target men in relationships are heavily deceived by the enemy because they think their manipulative ways can influence a man's heart. Earlier in the book we discussed the keepers of men. If a woman is not spiritually led she's either lead by her emotions, impulses or the enemy. So, here's a news flash; if you are romantically involved with a married man or a man who is committed, even if you are messing with a single man that God did not approve for you, I want to let you know that God is nowhere in that and He is not going to help you change anybody's heart from another woman to yours... or from the streets to yours, or from their singleness to yours. I've been there, I know. Settling for the at least is just that, settling, and you deserve so much better. In fact, better is ready for you, you just have to prepare for it! Take heart, that's exactly what you're doing now: preparing!

What You Need:

Ladies we must be diligent about discovering the character of a person prior to entering a relationship with them. As single women, it's important to burn the "at least" clause out of our vocabulary, and replace it with "the most "clause. By focusing on this clause, you highlight the greatest qualities that someone can offer you. We cannot afford to be involved with individuals who are not followers of Truth and don't have a spiritual life. Those who are dishonest or have no idea what it means to be faithful or loyal, people who are undeveloped, or self–centered... these types of people have no place in your life. When you become involved with these types of individuals you become connected to toxicity. Not that these people are bad people, God knows there can be wonderful things about them, but if someone is not ready, no matter how "good" they are, they will be no "good" for you! Guys who are undeveloped, ultimately desire to occupy their time with women in hopes of filling a void. This is not the man you need. They, just like you, gained their knowledge of love from the distorted examples displayed between their combination of family, friends and the media. When we entertain men, whose hearts are kept by themselves or the enemy, with a preconceived notion that the little bit of God in us has the power to change them, we are headed for disaster. We need men who are secure in who they are; strong leaders, grounded, kind, giving, timely, loving, and ultimately prepared.

Cautionary Tales

Ladies, while participating in the dating scene during our singleness there are several things that don't serve us, some of which we have already discussed but it never hurts to reemphasize this information. It's a lot to take in and can easily be forgotten at the sight of a handsome fellow. So, stay with me I got your back, and this book will serve as a direct and even challenging support system but, sometimes being nice doesn't cut it. Nice could not have been involved in my working process because I would have tip toed around real issues that I allowed to control my life in a negative way. There's nothing nice about the work but the payoff is beyond nice! It's rewarding...So let's continue.

#1: **It's dangerous for women to be the pursuer in their relationship**. Especially if she's unaware as to what is required of her as a result! I know you have heard this time and time again a man that finds a wife, not the other way around.

One thing I don't think women consider is that if you are the pursuer initially, your expected role will be that of the pursuer throughout the relationship. If you opt for this position it's unfair to assume that once you conquer the man it's his responsibility to do your part now that you're in a relationship. It rarely happens that way, especially without communication. While this concept falls under gender roles, if you decide to eradicate these roles from your relationship then don't get upset with a man if he fails to plan dates or call you first when you've been the one "responsible" for initiating that part of the relationship.

#2: **Women don't benefit from going along with relationships just for the sake of having one,** in an attempt to prove to a world, who could care less about her in the first place, that she's capable of having a man or to prove her self-worth or value.

#3: **It's unhealthy for women to seek companionship to fill voids.** This method will always leave you wanting more. We waste our singleness on pursing or being involved in dysfunctional relationships; neglecting our relationship with God, our family, and friends.

Next, I want to address a common saying among singles as it relates to how they should or should not conduct their relationships. Many of these sayings or beliefs we hold are used as a means to justify what we want to do but have no bearing on the plan already established for us.

The Common Saying: "Well it worked for my grandparents or parents"

Sometimes this works, sometimes it doesn't, especially if you aren't anything like your grandparents. It's your grandparents for crying out loud, they're from a different time. However, many women wonder why certain things worked for their grandparents and do not work for them. Many older couples that are married, where the wife has a clear spiritual life and the husband doesn't or vice versa, or both lack spirituality may have or have stayed married longer than people seeking marriage with those same descriptions in our generation, for many reasons. First and foremost, let's not forget, today women have just as many rights as men. With the inflation of women's rights, women are now able to maintain or in some cases do better financially as a single woman.

Secondly, our parents and grandparents' negative views about marriage and relationships, regardless if they are married or not, heavily influenced the way they taught the men and women of our generation about marriage and relationships.

Many of our grandparents disliked the marriage and relationship traditions that were instilled in them by their parents. To not pass those beliefs and traditions on, they made it their business to teach their children differently and as a result we are the ones who got the storage board of faulty marital advice. I have witnessed some older adults tell young men to "get it all out" "sow his wild oats" and other foolishness while pushing young women to practice purity and pursue an education. So, if all the boys are out here getting their rocks off, first who are they sleeping with and if you listened to your grandparents, what are you supposed to do...wait? I guess (with a side eye shrugging my shoulders)??? We can't ignorantly label this advice as wisdom. Moreover, we can't fail to mention the many men in our generation who grew up without father figures or proper male guidance. So, bless their hearts, many guys have no idea how to be a husband or a father. True wisdom comes from God, so while an older adult may share their experience, which may include a "lasting marriage" that defies God's design, we must be spiritually mature enough to filter the information and hold onto that which is good and discard that which is not. Grandparents, just like us, are people too and due to their negative experiences could taint the image God created for relationships and marriage, which may result in sharing unhealthy advice to singles.

On the contrary, sometimes our grandparents often share little nuggets of truth which we avoid in our attempt to do things our way. The key is wisdom and individuality, knowing the greatest individuals know how to decipher and absorb sound knowledge. All in all, the times are different and what worked for your grandparents and your parents may not hold up for you if you don't have the mind and heart of your grandparents or parents. Marriage isn't valued the way it used to be. People aren't willing to be long suffering the way they used to. Options are available through the scroll of a cellphone and the list continues as it relates to the number of distractions available to us that some of our elders would know nothing about.

The message I want to drive home is, ultimately the respect factor we should hold for our elders due to their experiences. Since they have experienced life in a way many of us haven't they possess a knowledge that is one of a kind. However, keep in mind the difference between wisdom and age-old foolishness. Age-old foolishness is just that, foolish. Now don't you be foolish enough to tell them that. Just remember, as in everything else we've discussed up until this point, hold tight to that which is good and discard the rest. Ladies just keep in mind if it worked for your grandparents, whatever it is, take their reaction, measure it to the direction of Truth, and make the application.

14

SEX

Should you Avoid Sex While You're Single

We live in a horny society, frankly speaking. We just want to have sex Bay-Bee and is that really a crime? The reasons vary: some want it to feel connected to someone, others desire to "please the man they're with", others use sex as a luring tactic to get what they want, and some people have a healthy sexual appetite. I confess, because everyone I knew was having sex and often bragged about how great it was, I wanted to give it a try. I was dating this senior in high school and he was good looking. He was already sexually active and I thought if I had sex with him he'd like me even more and possibly make me his girlfriend. Well none of that happened and in the middle of him pounding away at my teenage body I laid there thinking to myself: this is the dumbest idea ever. While this may not be your truth you know what your truth is. You remember your first encounter, be it by force or by choice, peer pressure or mere curiosity, that first time will never be forgotten. If you're anything like me you wish you could forget but it adds to your story and it really could be used to make you a better person.

At the time I lost my virginity nothing around me really helped deter me from making my decision except my mother. Most of my friends were active, the TV only showed people having sex who enjoyed it and men falling in love afterwards so I was frankly given a whole bunch of faulty material to help make the decision. Sex outside of marriage was the chief topic discussed at church of course but those people were so phony I ignored them because I needed them to practice what they preached first, then come for me. In my mind I rationalized, what could be the harm and since my mind was already made up, I already knew I was going to have sex and nobody could really do anything about it.

I lived a sexually charged existence for many years and seemingly to my demise one of the many lessons I later learned about sex was that those preconceived thoughts I had accumulated prior to my first encounter, coupled with the advice I received from peers, was the farthest thing from the truth. Gosh, I remember crying from the inside out the day I laid in his twin sized bed and handed him my virginity. Offering myself to someone that as of today I haven't seen or talked to in years and if I did see him I would probably snatch my virginity back and kick him in the face. Ha! If only it were that easy! Realistically speaking, if only it was his fault! I digress. From that day forward, I began the struggle with my sexual expression in an attempt to fill that void and achieve the moment that I saw in movie scenes.

I was praying to land that happy ending I saw women achieve but that moment never came. I later came to find the happy ending displayed on TV was just as bogus as the expectations of having a rewarding relationship with that young man I handed my virginity over to in a twin sized bed (I know right, twin sized). As a teenager, the media's display of happy endings was masked as truths in my mind. I discarded all the real-life information shared with me from family that warned me of the negative consequences of sex that include: soul ties, repeated disappointment, an attack of emptiness, the great likelihood of getting an STD, and countless other things. Yep, I ignored the truth that a guy could look me in the face, tell me he loved me and boldly continue having sex with multiple women. Why was one influence in my life greater than the other?

At that time, I had a superior respect for the things that appeased my emotions over the things that pleased my soul. The voice of reason and my best intentions were overpowered by what I allowed in my spirit, a strong force that had a for real influence over me. During that time the media and the music I loved was in heavy rotation throughout my spirit. The ratchet dancing and ideas of having a good time that I developed from popular opinion took over my thought life. The false ideas of what a relationship looks like, that I lusted after for years and advice from girls who I thought knew what they were talking about as it related to sex served as my chief source of guidance during this time. I based my decisions off my desire to have love and refused to accept that it was available to me at no cost; a concept I later figured out after I spent much of what I had.

Active Code

In the Christian community sex before marriage is a sin and has been officially but not legitimately proclaimed to be the second most worst sin after homosexuality. Neither of those are true, but it's one of those unspoken rules many Christians hold onto today. Personally, I think the whole sex before marriage topic is overly discussed among Christians and church folks. As a believer myself I'd be remiss if I didn't say that I 100% understand and value the principles of sex outlined in the Bible. I also understand that it was written for our protection and overall wellbeing. Despite the writer, the concept makes complete sense. As a woman who is no longer a virgin I understand the purity of abstinence and how abstaining from sex brings about clarity of mind, body, and spirit.

Likewise, as a woman who is no longer a virgin, I must admit that maintaining consistent abstinence is a struggle for me and in some seasons not a desire of mine at all. I understand that may not be the case for some women as everyone has different sexual drives and needs making abstinence more challenging for some rather than others. So, to be as transparent as possible with you, I want to speak my truth as well as biblical truths concerning this topic. Please know I wholeheartedly respect biblical principles and will always reverence God's truths at a higher level than my own thinking on any day. I daily ascribe to live my life according to His guidance. I will also have you to know as a result of my willful decision to defy everything that I believed as it relates to sex and God's design for relationships, I have suffered many consequences. I will also admit for years sex was not engaged in maturely and with meaningful intent a topic I will now further discuss.

When I lost my virginity, I gave no thought to it. I liked a guy, I wanted him to like me, I wanted to fit in, sex was an act of fitting in, so I had sex. There was nothing mature or meaningful to it; I just did it. My motives were not pure. My underlying hope was to get a guy to like me more than he already did. I thought sex would do that and in a way, I was being deceptive. Not only to the guy I had sex with but with myself as well. A truth I was only able to grasp as an adult. Highly disappointed in the result of my initial experience, I would, as stated earlier, continue having sex to obtain that magical feeling advertised by some family, friends, and the media; a dead-end journey. So, in my quest for this magic, that I already had inside just hadn't recognize it yet, I would give my body away to men in hopes that: 1) they'd like me, 2) to keep them interested in me/the relationship, and 3) because I was searching for a love and connectedness. Can we say this was indeed a recipe for disaster? Now according to the Bible, I was out of God's will because I engaged in sex without being married, a concept allowed by men in that same Bible but was always a travesty for women. I am in no way suggesting that God is/was pleased by the sexual immaturity of male biblical leaders I am just pointing out that the writers of the Bible spoke from the social standards of that time, where it was permissible for men to have several concubines and women to bathe themselves and smell good as they waited in these confined spaces to be chosen for sex by a man. What in the hell type of life is that, but whatever? Once again, I am not suggesting that God was cool with this at all, frankly I don't know. All in all, what I gather most from the Bible and even today, many people, especially people of power and men (even women who wanted to "get a man") engage(d) in sex meaninglessly and immaturely, even those who were married.

Say what? I know you are asking so here's what I mean. Personally, I know married women who admit to having sex with their husband for the same three reasons I admitted to giving my body away to men who weren't mine: 1) So they're husbands would like them. 2) To keep their husbands interested. 3) Because they are searching for love and connectedness. Not all married women have sex with their husbands for these reasons but the number of women who are, consciously or subconsciously, can be alarming. So, what was the true difference between me and those married women, a ring and documentation of a ceremony? Or was it that I lacked a covenant? Or would we be equal if one of the members in that covenant broke theirs, being that I never made one to begin with? Oh, and is that same covenant we make today the one they made in Bible days because if it is then... well I'm sure it's not because... well now I'm all confused. Well not really but it is confusing, right?

In my mind marrying a man that God never intended for you could be an act of operating outside of His will as well. Just as He can make that right can He not make us married-less women right who sleep with a man that isn't for us too? Because if He says something isn't right, there's nothing we can do to make it right...right? Not even a walk down the aisle...right? If I compare myself and the married woman who engage in meaningless and immature sex with her spouse, internally we are the same woman, battling the same issues. However, in religious society one person's truth is coined as a sin while the other person with the same issue is coined as not an issue at all because she's married? Then we can add in the topic of soul ties, but you know how many people are married to people with effed up souls. Like dark souls, pornographic souls, evil souls.

So, you're trying to tell me that if you're married to a person with a dark soul and you have sex with them that your soul won't be tainted or linked to darkness? I believe, and could be entirely wrong, that in God's eyes we are both damaged women looking for love in all the wrong places.

I will however admit that for me most of my sexual relationships were extremely damaging to my mind, body, and soul. I was looking for something in another person that they were never designed to give me and as a result I convinced myself that I could extract what I needed from them if I only gave them everything I thought, or what they verbalized, to have wanted. Some women may argue, they themselves enjoy sex and get equal benefit as that of the man they're sleeping with and as a woman who too enjoys sex I must say I can only admit to having few really great sexual partners, everyone else was truly a waste of my time. So, in the search for good sex I in return was losing myself. Due to all of this, I programed in my mind as it related to sex and the church and even God that because I was sinning I was unworthy of a relationship with Him. So, when I was younger and in my early twenties, I became ashamed of building my relationship with Him whenever I had sex; a flawed perspective that I still battle with today but ironically, it's only concerning that sin. If I'd be honest I could over indulge on pound cake but somehow rationalize that and pray at night. Or I could cuss someone (who deserved might I add) out but then ask for forgiveness as soon as the last profane word left my mouth, go home pray to God for myself and the other person and rest easy, but not with sex.

Every time I had sex I would turn away from God, sort of like Adam and Eve did after they ate the forbidden fruit; and why was that? In my life it wasn't because sex in totality was the issue or my forbidden tree, it was when He deliberately told me not to have sex with a particular person and I did it anyway, that bought about shame. Now, overly religious people would disagree suggesting that those feelings and that mindset I had after sex in general was a result of my sin. While I agree to some extent, I also believe that those feelings and that mindset was largely funneled by those same individuals who preached so hard against sexual sin but overlooked, or would often skirt past, all the other ones as if they were a lesser offense. Looking back, they seemed to be more confused than I was. Additionally, please note, it's a training of the mind that takes place in religious settings and as you begin to redefine your spirituality, you'll begin to readjust your thinking from religion to God.

So, I want to set the disclaimer: As a Christian I do believe that sex before marriage breaks religious law. Furthermore, I too believe that the misuse of sex in general is unhealthy regardless of you're married, single, engaged, dating...whatever. Anything that has the propensity to separate you from God is dangerous and may not send you to hell in the physical sense but it could create a mental or emotional hell for you. Distractions also naturally exposes you to things, emotions, and people who may be difficult or impossible to handle, as well as other physical and mental damage that could take years or lifetimes to eradicate. It's a tossup. You may get burned by the physical and mental consequences of sexual sin or you may not, but just like any other distraction, you further separate yourself from God. In my case, with men I knew I heard God say, "leave Him alone, or Kristen do not give your body away to this man" I was separating myself from the Father.

Now what about two individuals that do not desire marriage? Contrary to Christian opinion, I've met many people, (some even are believers) who have no desire to get married. Perhaps they were scorned by marital examples in their families or past. Maybe they were married before and was damaged as a result. Perhaps their reason is unknown or unexplainable, but they're in a committed relationship and hope to build a life together with their partner. Can this couple have sex? Sure, they can just like those of us who aren't in a relationship can have sex too, but is it right? Listen, we all have the liberty to do what's right for us. That is the greatest gift God gave us, free will. Optimally though, we want to ensure that our decisions in fact create freedom in our lives. Some people are in our lives just for a season but we abort their purpose when we try to make a lifetime out of the connection. If He says a thing we can rest in the fact that whatever He says is good. If He has a design in place, that design is for our good. If two people are sure they were made for each other, then they should follow God's leading as it relates to their lives and live freely. With that being said, I do believe that two consenting adults can engage in meaningful and mature sex without being married. Just as I believe two consenting married adults can have meaningless and immature sex. The decision to get married is personal and should not be glorified as the "right", or "justified", or "legitimized" thing to do. Healthy relationships in general is a good decision, period! Over the years the reason for, the meaning behind, and the intent of marriage has changed drastically. Regardless of those changes, don't allow rules or traditions to persuade or discourage you from what God is calling you to do in regard to your relationship status and future.

So where does that leave me as a single woman? It leaves me in a place where I should trust God. What does that look like? As of today, I will say I have started by being extremely intentional about who I date. I am always very prayerful about who is in my life and for what reason. I will continue to allow God to lead me as it relates to my relationships and what I do in them. Let's be honest, I could literally get married tomorrow. There are several men who'd marry me right now even; but is that what I truly desire? To have a husband I can have sex with to avoid the dirty looks and judgement of others? No, that's not for me and it's not for you either, as a matter of fact it's not for any of us. Yet we all know many women who settle in a marriage, just so they can express themselves sexually and be socially accepted. My advice is to do whatever pleases you but just try not to shackle yourself to a prison you weren't sentenced to.

God doesn't want you to get married to avoid dirty looks and judgements from others, so pay attention to your motives. All you can really do is love God with your entire being and trust Him. Trust that whatever the future holds is for your wellbeing and that He would never withhold any good thing from you. Understand His principles are true for you. Be intentional about allowing your relationship with Him to grow daily. I know that in this lifetime I have made many errors and will continue to mess up until the time I'm laid to rest. I know there will come a day when I have to give an account for my life. I know God knows me well and I also know these earthly battles will adjust over time.

To give a holistic approach to this topic I want to address the negative side effects of not only pre-marital sex but immature and pointless sex in general. When listing the benefits of sex, experts talk about how sex boosts your libido, decreases your likelihood of getting sick with common illnesses such as colds and viruses, lessens overall bodily pain, boosts your mood, and even counts as exercise. These experts somehow neglect to list the negative side effects of sex. Such as the negative effect sex can have on your health; both physically and mentally until people start dying. You might be able to cure some STDs with medication but it takes an act of God to heal a broken heart. The longer you live with a broken heart and the more times your one heart continually breaks, that heart will become hard and jaded. This causes any person who tries to love you to become hurt because of your hurt. This applies to both single and married women. I'm not sure where this notion comes from that assumes a marriage will erase a person's brokenness or wayward heart. Many people, especially in this generation, get married for the wrong reasons. Men and women are marrying people who are not for them and I want you to understand that God is not pleased with them either. We often confuse the church community with God and that's the furthest thing from the truth. When we do that we displease Him as well. As a means of control, many religious communities overstep their boundaries into the lives of others who've already been accounted for through the blood of Jesus.

Much of the arguments Christians engage in have already been handled on the cross but in an effort to make oneself appear better than the other they nitpick at the sins of others, often the sins they claim to have overcome. Like it kills me how married men and women bark at singles for having sex. Um sir or ma'am that husband or wife is the same boyfriend or girlfriend you were sleeping with so hush. Or you waited but if you were really honest, like real honest, the type of stuff people discuss on my couch or in a prayer closest you're unhappily married and your sex life sucks. Not saying this is true for all marriages but more often than not the truth is not always what it appears to be. Don't fall into the trap of condemning yourself about your "sin", single ladies. *"All have sinned and come short of the glory of God"*. Romans 3:23

Since you're grouped in the "all", it looks like you are in good company. Thank God for Jesus!

A thought provoking approach or wisdom to help you be your best self is helpful but anything other than that just doesn't serve you. Be confident in who you are and let God guide your life, not some overzealous Christian person, who preaches against everything Christ taught anyway. You will make mistakes; this is not a pass to just live life recklessly, just a mere fact! No one is sinless except the Father so in this life you will have struggles, and your struggles are a reminder that you need Him. I want to make it very clear that if you were to marry a man with the uncommunicated expectation that he'll love you, or be faithful to you, or that he'll treat you better, you're opening yourself up to a slew of heart breaks and heartaches that as a married woman you can't easily walk away from. Whereas a single woman, sex or no sex, you have the option to walk away when you're not getting what you need. Some people hold the belief that if they get married all will be well with them because they can legitimately have sex.

This is the reason God created boundaries for sex. While many people limit these boundaries to single people, overall, He doesn't want any of us giving ourselves away to the wrong person. If you make the decision to marry the wrong person that decision does not automatically make that person or the situation right. Giving yourself away to the wrong people will leave you with a hardened heart, skewed views about relationships, soul ties and much more. That's why He established those barriers and safeguards prior to our existence. Not to limit us, but to guide and protect us. Ladies, God loves us immensely, He is our first love. The world has given us the idea that we can do anything that makes us temporarily happy. Yet, it fails to give us the full picture, including the end result of those temporary decisions. Moreover, this world's view is not designed to protect our hearts. The idea of having it all and doing you own thing gives us a license to be constantly self-destructive, always searching, yet never fulfilled. The world's tactics are not designed to protect you against being connected to a person that was never divinely destined to be a part of your life; single or married. Also, I want to add this, yes, you can be connected to a person without sexual activity but with sex in the picture, you have a greater likelihood of putting up with so much more than you typically would in a sexless relationship.

It has been observed that "good girls" will stay with the wrong guy just because they've had sex with them and why do you think they do that? Let's be honest, single women make this decision to uphold that good girl image. You can't be a good girl around here giving it up all Willy-Nilly they say. The unspoken rule for women is three guys tops before marriage, or at least that's the lie you "ought to tell". To do a really good job of keeping those numbers down, good girls often put up with just about anything from a guy simply because they've had sex with him. As if God is going to punish you based of the number of men you slept with. Girl **please**, one man to God is like 1,000. According to religious law it's a sin, no one is greater than the other, and it can be forgiven! I want to be clear, I am not suggesting that you start having sex with multiple men because God isn't keeping tally of your numbers, or that you should keep ignoring Him and slapping a "He'll forgive me on it", what I am saying is, if you are having sex with man #1, 2, 3, 4, 5, 6 or beyond you don't have to stay with a person who is not for you simply to avoid being called loose or for fear of racking up your number of sexual partners. You are not obligated to a man because you've had sex with him; you are obligated to live your best life with God's guidance. Don't get me wrong, sleeping around comes with consequences. It opens you up the possibility of you being labeled as a whore, baby daddy(s), vaginal issues, you'll spread yourself thin, many people will be able to say, "they had you", and you'll create much internal damage...mentally and physically. However, God is not in heaven like "Did you see that? She's sleeping with guy #15 tonight." He's just heartbroken for you, that you don't understand your value and His plan!

Abstinent Code

Next, we will address abstinence. Let me start by saying how proud you should be of yourself and your decision but more importantly

God is proud and heaven is smiling. This decision shows God that you're willing to eliminate your distractions so you can hear Him. Being abstinent is also a method of purification. By abstaining from sex, you are purifying yourself from all the emotional chaos that is attached to sex and that is a liberating experience! You just think clearer while abstaining, don't you? You have no idea the number of women that ask me if I think a man will stay around if they tell him their plan to wait for marriage and quite frankly, does it even matter? If he doesn't, *forget* him, the one God has for you will. I wasn't always so sure though.

I thought my past would in some way impact God's decision. I was not all the way positive that God cared enough about me to send me a good man. I was convinced that because I was relationship-less that God had forgotten all about me. However, as I developed my relationship with Him, I came to understand that me and my wellbeing is always on His mind and He will not withhold anything good from me. *Psalms 84:11 "For the Lord God is our sun and our shield. He gives us grace and glory. The*

LORD will withhold no good thing from those who do what is right".

I may not meet the future hubby tomorrow, next year, or five years from now but God gave me many promises and I believe Him.

1. He will not withhold any good thing from me (I must stand on that one)

2. He will give me the desires of my heart

3. It is not good for man to be alone

4. If I abide in Him and His words abide in me I can ask for whatever I want and it will be given to me and last, but not least, in my case;

5. God has given me many specifics about my husband and I can't wait to meet him and see all this wonderfulness in the natural. That part really excites me.

I know God to be honest. I know man to lie. Therefore, I place all bets on Him. Let's take an

Understanding Moment and get to the root of things before we move forward. Understand this: Spirituality is a practice of faith. Do you have faith? Yes or No. It's that simple. We try to over complicate it and it's a simple yes or no question. Do I trust that the sun rises at some point in the day and the moon comes forth at night? Yes, I do. How it all happens is beyond me but I know it will happen regardless if I can see it or not. Two things are certain the sun shines during the day and the moon lights up the night. Do I trust that within me lies thousands of eggs and these tiny eggs when connected with one sperm create little people? Yes, I do. Can I explain to you how bones, cartilage, muscle, eyes, hair, fingers, and nails are inside those eggs? I surely cannot yet regardless of my inability to fully explain or understand it, I do believe it. So, can I explain to you everything about God so that you can fully comprehend and understand it? No, I cannot. God's ways are not like mine, nor are His thoughts. I can only share with you what He tells me and trusts Him to make it all make sense to you. In the same sense, can I explain to you everything about myself? No way, I am still a work in progress. Can you explain everything about your parents, the guy you like, or even yourself?

No, you cannot but we somehow develop full faith in them, especially men we are romantically involved with. We have faith they are not harboring any deadly STD's, that they are not really an ax murderer, and that their number one goal is to make us happy and we act on that faith by pursing a relationship with them. With all this unexplainable certainty there's still that part that doesn't allow us to trust the **ONE** who makes it all possible. God is a giving God; He's a comforter and help in times of trouble.

The enemy is the one who causes all confusion, he condemns, and he sets people up for failure. Not Truth, not the Divine Spirit who has your back, always. Look at the Garden of Eden. The devil acted as the serpent luring Eve with a good thing, fruit. Just like sex, sex is a good thing, but when done with the wrong person... it's extremely problematic. As soon as Eve ate the forbidden fruit, as soon as you have sex with that loser here comes the enemy, condemning you and making you feel unworthy for even going there in the first place. It's a trap. Trusting God with your relationships and your body is all that He requires of us. That's pure trust. Certainly, once we develop our trust in Him, He can fully work in our lives.

As, juvenile as this may sound, the only way to keep those lines of communication open with your Creator and to remain in that space of clarity and direction, is to continue being daddy's little girl and dwell with Him instead of some guy who doesn't even qualify to be in your dwelling place anyway. You are never too old to be God's baby girl and as silly as it sounds it's the God's honest truth. That silly little saying will save you from many heart aches, pains and children with less than ideal fathers too. So good job! For all my ladies who are struggling with having sex with men who are undeserving, let's keep it real, once that cat is out the bag it's difficult to chase it down and confine it again. The cat is safe as long as you are not around a man that could potentially get it. Hence abstinence! However, there may be an animal in trouble the moment you meet someone you enjoy. When you get that feeling that runs through your entire body, it's going to take more than a repetitive "I think I can, I think I can, I think I can" to keep you out of the sheets.

If your goal is abstinence you must infuse your mind, body, and soul with why abstinence is beneficial prior to temptation to help you resist when the time comes. You need to be honest with men about your decision for abstinence and be serious about it. I've learned, from my own past, it's difficult to redeem yourself when you start off preaching abstinence on Day 3 of meeting someone yet on Day 23 you can't get the two if you out of the bedroom. You will be taken as a joke and will not be able to redeem yourself, trust me on this one. If you are not sure if you can wait until marriage be honest. Share your thoughts at the appropriate time and be confident that with God all things are possible. I don't want to mislead you as if it will be an easy temptation to resist; you have to be serious and willing to do the work. God is not going to put a 'horny blocker' on your hormones. He tried to stop you before you let the cat out the bag, but you didn't listen and He is not a God that makes us do anything, so now it's your turn. He loves you enough to give you the opportunity to grow and make the right choices for YOU! If you're deliberate about putting in the work to show Him you're serious, trust me, He'll do his part.

On the other hand, some single women are so jaded by sex or the world's views of sex, they have no idea the value God placed on sex. I tell people all that time that sex is worship, and they think I am crazy. I tell them about my desires to have pleasurable sex when I get married and they tell me I shouldn't verbalizes that or tell that to God. Why not? We have haphazardly taken a God ordained act and handed it over to the enemy, gave him the glory for it, and in return view sex as a negative act. For some reason people think sex is a topic that should not be discussed even in decency, and that is because we have abused it. God created sex. Everything He creates is good and very good might I add, and when not abused, immature, or meaningless we'll receive the lasting benefits of sexual relationships.

When you Fall

It's important to me that I am as authentic as I can be with you. That's why I'm so open about sharing my journey, my struggles, what I do to "keep me on track", **when** I'm on track, etc. Initially, it was as if, I had to put myself in a mental boot camp to motivate me away from the sheets. In Christendom I believe we set up unforgiving barriers for sin regarding everyone else. We take on the pompous attitude that my sins can be forgiven but yours can't. Well I want to assure you that everyone can be forgiven... that includes the woman who goes against her commitment to abstain from sex and engages in the act despite her decisions and conviction. Kristen Black will not lie to you; she has fallen and honestly, at times, purposefully walked into a sexual situation during an abstinence sabbatical. Personally, this is a delicate topic for me because meaningless and immature sex was once a very real struggle for me and because of that being my truth, I have come to learn there are many women who struggle with meaningless and immature sex as well and I want to address some of the various reasons.

There is the **Abused Woman**: The abused woman has experienced some type of sexual abuse in her lifetime either from a family member, friend, was exposed to sex at an early age, has been raped, and so forth. Sex, a gift from God, has been wrongfully exposed to and/or forced upon her.

Next, we have the **Insecure Woman**: This woman engages in sex because she is struggling with insecurities. She may have grown up as the ugly duckling, struggles with her own emotional battery, or rarely receives recognition from men so when one shows her attention she sleeps with him as a means of acceptance. She may want to feel loved, even if she knows it isn't real love, that temporary moment of sexual gratification satisfies her longing for connection. This woman may also feel like she will never be in a relationship, or that she is not good enough to be loved by a man. She then, makes the decision to takes matters into her own hands and attempts to control her love life, which almost always ends in pointless sexual relationships.

Finally, we have the **Hurt Woman**: She has been hurt by men, perhaps her father or male figure in her life, in relationships, in a failed marriage, etc. so she takes control of her sexual freedom and finds validation in her ability to control her body.

God views all sins the same and while I will

never attempt to be God or play God, or act like God I do have a soft spot for why people do what they do, and I know God does too. He is all gracious and loving, wanting nothing but the best for us. I was once the insecure woman, the hurt woman, and the abused woman. Early in my singleness that insecure woman in me liked to pop her ugly head up and throw me totally off my game. As a woman who suffers with insecurities, life for you can be hard. I will even venture to say, it's harder for you than others. The reason could be you, never having felt good enough or confident enough in any area of your life. This affects you professionally, personally, and relationally. Even when you have given it your best shot, (in some cases performing better than the others), that insecure woman in you pops up and finds a way to devalue you.

The insecure woman ends up in the bed with men because she is unable to understand her worth. She may even know that she is valuable but for whatever reason is hindered from fully grasping it. She is often the hopeless romantic, wanting to date one man at a time all in hopes of becoming his wife. This man may not be good for her and she may know that completely.

However, the presence of a man or just that mere sign of affection can make that insecure woman feel valued, wanted and loved.

Singe ladies, I just want to encourage you that no one is quarantined from sin. Everyone has that one area or more they struggle in that takes much work to overcome. No one is too good to be tempted by the enemy or humbled by God. You just may fall into or walk into sexual sin! Nevertheless, let me assure you that you are not a bad person. God does not revoke his love for you when you sin, you will not fall straight to Hell when you sin, and your life is not doomed when you sin. If so we would ALL be in Hell for one reason or another. Consequences may transpire but God is still the same sovereign God who loves you unconditionally. Now please understand me, should you just keep sinning because our loving God is going to forgive you? Please no, that's equivalent to abuse. Just live your life the best way you know how and know even when you mess up it doesn't mean that you aren't trying, unless you simply aren't.

Just to break the concept down a step further; let's say, you have perfect attendance at work. You are always on time and ready to give your entire self to your workday. However, this past Monday you were late to work because you accidently locked yourself out of your car. When you got to work your boss said, "Its ok, things happen". On Thursday you were late too because traffic was awful. You left a little later that normal but if it had not been for the traffic you would have made it exactly on time. Your boss looks at you again and says, "I understand, that was a horrible accident and things happen". Friday night you go out with some friends and wake up Saturday morning terribly tired. You have to be to work in the morning, but you choose to sleep in and arrive to work late because you are tired. At this point, you are taking advantage of the system. You have been late to work two times without any consequences, after all you are never late anyway, then you decided to take you own liberty and show up to work when you felt like it. You are taking advantage of your boss's kindness to appease your desires.

The same happens with God. When you keep sinning and start to become lax in your standards you begin to take advantage of God's kindness to appease your desires. Yes, He forgives us when we ask but when we just keep doing it and abusing His forgiveness, then we have a problem. The biggest problem is you have allowed yourself to be exposed to circumstances and problems that you could have avoided. There is so much more to learn in this life and the quicker you get the lesson the quicker you can move on!

My best advice for the faller, or the purposefully walker inner, is to take this journey one day at a time. You may never get it right. I know for me that idea is a problem because I get so upset when I do not pass the test and just get it, but the truth is you may never. You may die struggling with sexual sin. But God delights in the struggle. When He sees your efforts, He rewards you. When He sees you pressing towards the mark He favors you. When He sees you saying "F" it I have a problem God, deal with it (in word, in deed, or in heart) He becomes angry. He feels used and taken advantage of. He feels ignored and unappreciated. So, avoid that and take it one day at a time. Do everything in your power to avoid sex with men who are unworthy of you and if you fall get up and draw nearer to God. Do not pull away; He is not mad at you He simply wants you to come to Him so he can restore you and place you right back on the path of greatness.

"Cast your cares on Jesus". 1 Peter 5:7

"Are you tired? Worn out? Burned out on religion? Come to me. Get away with me and you'll recover your life. I'll show you how to take a real rest. Walk with me and work with me— watch how I do it. Learn the unforced rhythms of grace. I won't lay anything heavy or ill-fitting on you. Keep company with me and you'll learn to live freely and lightly." Matthew 11:28-30 (The Message)

Virgin Code

I want to dedicate this next section to all virgins. If you are not a virgin, please do not skip this section. Take this information and pass it along to other young girls or women you know who still have their virginity. You may even want to hide these truths in your heart as you rededicate your body to Christ and abstain from sexual activity.

Let me begin by saying kudos to you! You have held on to your virginity and I encourage you to continue holding on. God has a promise for those who obey and trust Him. I want to unveil some truths as it relates to keeping your virginity. Making the decision to keep your virginity will in no way protect you from natural life occurrences. Those seemingly bad things that may happen that were predestined prior to our existence. It also does not guarantee that you will have a happy marriage if you wait. Sex is an added bonus to any marriage; it is not the primary fundamental component, or the part of a marriage that should carry the most weight. You may get a guy who is willing to wait for you, but his character may be extremely flawed, he could be using you as a rebound, or to mask his inadequacies. It is also possible, he may not even have the slightest clue as to who he is or what he's even supposed to be doing in life and countless other characteristics that screams he isn't the one for you, so don't be fooled. Lastly your value is not attached to your sexual status. I know you may be wondering, so what is the point of waiting? First and I hope foremost, your ultimate desire is to please God and/or to avoid meaningless or immature connections with random people, who hinder your growth. If, your desire to maintain your virginity is linked to your self-worth or to please some man you will experience many complex things such as problems, great disappointments, and total futility. Men are simply creations of God, not gods, so therefore we cannot focus on pleasing the creation and not the Creator. Though it may appear that we are pleasing the Creator because it is a virtue of His, your motives have the ability to taint that virtue.

Wow, that was A Lot Right! Take a breather and review the scriptures located in the first few chapters. These are scriptures I used during my process of learning. I shared them with you so you could have the opportunity to read and reread them for understanding using a version of the Bible that is easiest for you to understand. I recommend the NLT or The Message version; NKJV and The Amplified are great resources as well. The versions used in this book are all from the NLT version or The Message. I also recommend comparing multiple versions and writing what you understood from each. This will help you get into the habit of doing a personal bible study. Personal bible studies teach you how to find scripture, helps you become familiar with the books of the Bible and their locations as well as understanding God and what He has to say about your life. As you go through the scriptures write what you gain from each verse and spend time dwelling there.

15

Peace in your Singleness

Creating a Life You Love

If you search for peace, I am a believer you will find it. I am a living witness too. As single women we experience so many conflicting thoughts and emotions. There are societal pressures which remind you that by now you should be (whatever society deems necessary for you to be), family asking about boyfriends, babies, rings, etc., friends that flaunt their fruitless relationships in your face, and your own personal quest to find meaningful relationships. You spend money you don't have to get new clothes to go out in, to go places you don't have fun at anyway, on hair and makeup that sometimes is overdone, all so you can look presentable for a man you may or may not run into. I know some single women are probably saying I don't do all of that to find a man, I do it for myself. Well, can you honestly say if a good looking man approached you and complimented you on your looks, you'd be upset about him acknowledging your efforts? Sure, you may not be doing it for him but it wouldn't hurt if he noticed.

With that said, unfortunately, peace just doesn't magically occur in our lives. I wish there was a 1-2 step formula I could share with you that would automatically bring peace, but there just isn't anything out there. Even when I reached a point in my life where a had developed my personal relationship with God and was even writing this book, I still hadn't fully found peace in my singleness. I was still out here looking for new crushes and one day it hit me; I was lying in bed and God was like "are you done now"? He actually went in on me and proceeded to ask, "what in the world would make you think I don't have the best for you, Kristen". "I know you, I know your ways. I know your desires, why wouldn't your future husband be compatible with that"? So, I released my relationship status! I had to ask God for peace and wait for it to come. Right now, I am challenging you to do the same. It may take some time depending on where you are on your journey. Or considering the stipulations you've put in place for God but once you fully release that area to Him, He will give you peace. When you get peace, you understand life more. Not the details but simply how it works. When you get peace, you gain trust. When you get peace, God can finally work in your life without interruptions. There is peace in singleness; and I'll have you to know, getting a man or into a relationship, even getting married, won't automatically guarantee peace in your life. You have to cultivate peace in your singleness and work hard at cultivating it in your marriage as well.

Single & Satisfied

So far, we have discussed a lot as it relates to being single. We've explored our past, our upbringings, our family, morals, values, etc. We have talked about sex, dating, abstinence and building a good relationship with God. We have discussed both our friendships and relationships. We have answered questions, read scriptures and filled ourselves with a plethora of information as it relates to being a single woman.

In this final section, we are going to tie all the information together and discuss a type of woman who I'd classify as single and satisfied. From this point forward, I will refer to her as *"The Committed Single Woman"*.

Women who are on the quest of becoming committed in the form of a relationship, often fail to practice being committed to themselves. To reach this level of singleness, one should complete the foundational work in their lives and become serious about continuing that work daily. For example, *The Committed Single Woman* doesn't wait until she gets into a relationship to do this. She understands the value of consistently committing herself to becoming a better and more well-rounded woman. How can one commit themselves to this process? You must vow to put your wellbeing first and be intentional about the decisions concerning your life. *The Committed Single Woman* is a woman who also understands the necessity of singleness and is determined to maximize that season of her life. While she has a desired relationship status, which could be to remain single or one day get married, she submits her life to God and lives boldly anyhow. With this renewed mindset she understands first, that God honors her commitment to Him. Secondly, she believes the desires of her heart and more will be given to her as she maintains her trust in God, not in her own ability. Her number one desire is to develop her relationship with the God-head first. She understands that this relationship creates a greater understanding of herself and provides direction for her future. Tired of the façade used to appear righteous on the outside, *The Committed Single Woman* desires to live authentically and true to her own identity. She knows that this mindset results in healthy relationships all around. To be her best self, she constantly searches her motives and heart for everything she does, prays for, and desires. She seeks to understand her reasoning for desiring a relationship and she puts her single life into perspective.

So you can accomplish this in your life, it's wise to determine your own motive for wanting a romantic relationship. Are you fearful of being alone or are you seeking partnership for more divine reasons, such as legacy building purposes? Patience with yourself is key here. There is nothing like being aware of your own readiness for meaningful relationships. When you're ready, mastery isn't the obligation. Being conscious of your communication skills and becoming in touch with your feelings and practicing how to control them, is the goal. *The Committed Single Woman's* goal is to be in alignment; fully tapped into who she is and what she offers. She is determined to be the woman God called her to be, even if that means no man, no ring, no promotion, no job and no money. That is *The Committed Single Woman!* She is committed to God and trusts that He will supply all her needs according to His riches in glory. It took me 25 years to realize who she was.

I Want to be Her

I cannot stress enough how vital it is to develop yourself as a single woman. I promise it will make you a better person and help you build and nurture your one-day marriage. People often want to skip over the developmental stage and immediately enter into holy matrimony which, more often than not, leads to difficult relationships. *The Committed Single Woman* is prepared for marriage because she understands that marriage consists of two whole people, who are fused together by God to make one. She understands that Christ acts as the bonding fluid that creates permanent adhesion between herself and her future husband. She has learned that marriage becomes problematic when she takes ½ of herself and ½ of some man and attempt to put them together. If you don't believe that, try it yourself. Cut a ball or something round in half. Here's an aside: In our lives everything that has happened is sure to come around again, as we continue living. Marriages have good times and bad times but if you keep going around you will eventually get back to those good times. This will give you hope when bad seasons resurface. That's how we grow.

So, take something round. Cut it in half and try putting it back together. How did it go? Are you having difficulty keeping it together? Sure, you are! You have a mess on your hand for three reasons. 1) Who did the cutting? You did. 2) Who put it together? You did. 3) How is it staying together? You are either holding it or you are using a manmade material so it can become whole again. That method may work but only temporarily. We should understand the same principle applies to relationships. We have to be intentional about offering our whole selves and not just half of us because when we only offer pieces we offer dysfunction!

Understanding Wholeness

Ladies, when you come into a relationship with half of you it signifies that the other half of you is someplace else. Where could it be? Well, because of your past, some of you could be left in previous relationships. Some parts of you may be left in past hurts and countless other places that you've totally forgot about. In the interim, while you may not be able to piece it all together, you may be aware that something is missing. Subconsciously, we often fill those missing spaces with useless relationships, material things, jobs, money, or busyness. With that, there is often an underlying component to such behaviors that damages us from the inside out.

This component results in fear, anger, worn out emotions, frustrations, and even a bad attitude, all chipping away at the part of you that's left. With all that, do you really think you are ready for healthy relationships or better yet a husband? Marriage is not the time to begin working on yourself. The time to get yourself together is when you are single. The *Committed Single Woman* understands that.

Is the *Committed Single Woman* a perfect person, never failing, doubting or making a mistake? No! No one is perfect, but she pursues perfection daily. She strives to be the best person she can be while giving her relationship with God 100% of her effort. Can you now see how these character traits will be beneficial when you become married? You'll need to have the same mindset if you're seeking health in your relationship status. You can't decide to be a wife 15% Mon- Thurs, 88% Friday and 61.7% Saturday and Sunday. You must make strides to be a loving, committed wife 100% of the time, seven days a week. Taking it a step further, after you walk down the aisle is not the time to begin knowing and understanding your spouse. This is why courtship is necessary! We live in a backwards society, which yields backward results! We wonder why marriages, families, children, and people are destroyed. It's because adult men and women have failed to seek holistic living and aren't purposeful during their singleness.

A *Committed Single Woman* understands the areas she needs to work on daily during her singleness. She builds her relationship with God, (I cannot stress this enough), she works on her communication skills at work, with friends, and family. She also monitors her attitude, tests her willingness to listen and her ability to accurately process information. The *Committed Single Woman* calls out her selfishness and pride, and daily practices patience. Another thing I have noticed about the *Committed Single Woman* is her determination to understand what love is. Our society would define love as an unidentifiable emotion that has no definition and is subject to the feeler. Well, 1 Corinthians 13:4-7 says the complete opposite.

"Love is patient and kind. Love is not jealous or boastful or proud ⁵or rude. It does not demand its own way. It is not irritable, and it keeps no record of being wronged. ⁶It does not rejoice about injustice but

rejoices whenever the truth wins out. [7] *Love never gives up, never loses faith, is always hopeful, and endures through every circumstance"*. NLT

If you spend time understanding and living out this love, I know you will be ready to both love and experience love healthily. This is no fly by night understanding, it's a process. You have your work cut out for you on this one. I promise! But as the *Committed Single Woman* learns to love, she commits herself to developing who she is at the same time.

16

Being Single Has a Purpose

Making Sense of it All

I N order to become a *Committed Single Woman* there are a few more areas we need to discuss. What better way to put everything we've talked about thus far into perspective, than to identify your purpose? Everyone has a purpose in this life. I would hate to leave this world without knowing or even tapping into my mine. Purpose has a weird way of defining itself for everyone. Some people were born just to give a part of their body so that a sibling, loved one or even a total stranger could live. Why? I am in no way skilled to explain the uncertainties of life. Solomon said it best in Ecclesiastes 11. Some people's purpose is to die so that others may see Christ through their death. I know that's scary business but don't be frightened or alarmed it's all to God's glory. It is simply just one of the many uncertainties that we may never understand. While, I consider this odd to share I consider my purpose in life to die so that others may live. Not in the natural sense, but in the flesh. I will share a quick story with you about me.

I knew my calling was for women and children when I was 12 years old. I told God there is no way I wanted that type of responsibility at that age because it would require me to live a set apart life. What is a set apart life? A life that does not go along with the crowd and denies my natural urges to do what I wanted to do. I boldly told Him "no, go ask someone else" because I did not want to do it, eventually adding "maybe later" to the story. God is not the forceful type but He will alter your circumstances to bring you closer to Him and boy did He! I began to search for my worth and value in men. Growing up with a single mother, I wanted that missing link in my life. I needed it. I had no earthly idea God, was the missing piece I needed. My mother was a Christian for most of my life, so I knew what God required of me. I just was afraid to truly trust Him because I felt He wanted me to live a restricted lifestyle. Well, in my quest for freedom to do what I wanted to in life I learned that the world had more restrictions than I had bargained for. I wanted a meaningful relationship, but a meaningful relationship didn't want me. So, to be accepted by those who I felt could give me this relationship, in my 15 year old mind, having sex with them would certainly increase that possibility. I wanted to party and hang with friends in my neighborhood, so I limited myself to that tiny, immature, unenlightened circle. Had I listened to the Lord there is no telling where I could have been instead. In my effort to escape God's limitations I placed limitations on God's power in my life and remained stuck, for years but was it really stuck, or a place of learning?

Could it have been exactly where I was supposed to be? It seems you never get the gold until it is fired up!

While you are single there is no better time to ask that your purpose be revealed to you. Once you discover what it is, it's imperative that you hop on board immediately to avoid wasting any more time. When I finally listened to God and started a women's empowerment group in 2011, I had $45 in my regular account, zero connections, and no formal training on where to start. But one thing I knew I had, was a sure foundation. I could count on this foundation to stabilize me during my growth. I stepped out on faith and doors opened. We had catered luncheons for women discussing topics that plague the 21st century woman; we had a male panel relationship advice event at an Atlanta restaurant. We had two fashion shows with two nationally known department stores, a summer program for homeless and displaced children and the list continues of the many accomplishments experienced by the organization within its first year. All with a calling and $45. I say all this to encourage you. The time to figure out your purpose in life and start pursuing it is while you are single with zero distractions. Especially, if you don't have any children and aren't dating. You have plenty of time to figure it out and get moving. If you are a single mother, instead of using all your energy longing to have a man, take that energy and desperate longing for companionship and live out your life's purpose for the benefit of you and your child(ren).

Also, for the women actively dating, it's not beneficial to reserve all your free time for dates. Utilize the open time slots in your schedule to maximize your life. How much time do you spend developing those other relationships we talked about earlier in the book; your spiritual relationship, your relationship with your family and even friends? Being involved in a relationship does not suggest "replacement time". Replacement time is when most of your available time is replaced with your new relationship. This is so unhealthy, and it really limits your personal growth as well as hinders your relationships with others.

When we become overly focused on our interpersonal relationships we often neglect our spiritual development. If you are with someone who demands all your free time you may want to reconsider this person. The people in your life should push you towards your destiny, encourage you to develop and sustain a well-rounded support system, and inspire you internally. If you continually fall victim to "replacement time" you my friend must master the art of balancing to be successful in *all* your relationships. The balancing act is basically when you strategically balance your life to include everything you need, want, and love.

Let me also add because I understand, there are some women who choose to date multiple people. It's important to understand that while you are dating and developing who you are, that you begin assessing what works for you and what doesn't. While doing this, you'll also have to learn to be ok with whatever you find out; careful not to force issues, people or situations. Let things flow naturally and allow what works for you to work and get rid of the rest. Dating and courtship is a crucial period and it is extremely necessary to become centered during that time. Being very aware and intentional while dating and courting promotes maturity and depth to your relationships and it helps you become the best woman you can be.

This ultimately makes an experience with you similar to a breath of fresh air, allowing others to see the true essence of a well-rounded and healthy woman, inside and out. Knowing what works for you and what doesn't, helps you handle and properly see distractions and people, as well as help you identify temptations. It allows you to define the direction of your relationships and become clear about suitable durations for specific individuals. Contrary to popular opinion, every "good" and "decent" person you meet may not be for you or will only be in your life for a limited time. We meet people daily who may be a better fit for someone else, such as a friend or family member. However, it's hard to identify that, if we're self-absorbed and struggling with self-assurance issues. The key is being patient, understanding that what's for you is for you. And to not try to fit a round peg into a square hole...

To recap, we have discussed the many ways the *Committed Single Woman* spends her free time: 1) developing her spiritual relationship, 2) improving herself, and 3) identifying her purpose. Next, we will explore the *Committed Single Woman* and her friends.

Friendships & Committed Singleness

As a *Committed Single Woman,* it's important to understand the significance of establishing friendship before romantic partnership. When meeting someone who interests you romantically, instead of leading with your emotions learn to lead with clear direction. Ladies, let's be real, whether you are single or married you will encounter all types of attractive people. It is necessary to understand what a friendship with someone you're attracted to looks like and the healthy boundaries that should be established. We talked about this earlier in the book so this information isn't totally new to you. You must be mature enough to search a man's motives for wanting your friendship or your motives for wanting his and understand the limits you need to establish because of that clarity. You also should be willing to enforce those limits utilizing self-control. So let's suppose, you meet someone you are interested in: (**LISTEN**- *there is no need to rush into a relationship. To help you slow down a bit, remember what we discussed earlier: what's for you is already yours)* By leading with this mindset, you allow yourself to comfortably take the time to get to know the person and what they're about. If you must remind yourself of this every now and again, it's ok. No need to be ashamed, we reinforce self-discipline by reminding ourselves to slow down.

Emotions have the tendency to cloud judgement and understanding the art of pacing yourself helps build effective strategies of communication. Communication that helps you gauge things, like how they interact with family, and question if those behaviors are suitable for the family you hope to one day have. You will learn how they interact with strangers and how you can analyze their life goals to determine if your goals are aligned. You will discover the important parts that create a complete picture and determine what that picture really is. For example, you'll determine if it's a romantic or platonic picture. Another thing you may want to consider is how he treats the elderly or disabled.

Sis, God forbid something happens and you become disabled, or when you get a little older, how will he treat you? Observe the way he treats God and himself. If he can't respect himself or God what makes you think he will continue to respect you? Watch how he spends and saves his money, watch his work ethic, watch, learn, and take time to understand this man in totality. After all, being involved with him directly affects you. Furthermore, understanding who he is does not mean you should agree with it or continue developing an intimate relationship. Understanding, allows you to see exactly what's in front of you, so you can make the best possible decision, concerning who you invite into your life and to what degree.

Here is the silent no brainier: People are getting divorced left and right, because they are not establishing friendships first. They meet someone they like on the surface and immediately pursue a serious relationship with a complete stranger. I believe they have every intention of getting to know the person throughout the relationship but that innocent plan almost always falls through because of emotions, sex, hope, desire and premature feelings. Behaviors that should raise question are overlooked, confronting certain topics, avoided, and the genuine nature of either person is masked by who they aspire to be. It has been said that when you meet a person you meet their representative, but is that representative truly flawed? Not necessarily. I believe a person's representative is who they wish to be, which can also be explained as the best version of themselves. To be honest, being your best self consistently is hard to maintain if you haven't developed a habit of putting it into practice daily. All the above, unaddressed, contributes to relationship failure!

By paying attention to a man's habits you

will learn his decision-making abilities. If he struggles making everyday decisions what makes you think he can make decisions in your home? If he's always running after the next best thing while accomplishing nothing in the pursuit, have you ever considered that he may one day want to upgrade you if emotionally he becomes a little too uncomfortable or even bored. All this to remind you that we usually end up with the wrong man because we're either mesmerized by the representative or too intrigued by who they told us they were, overlooking the obvious.

On the opposing side, some women become involved with men who require them to be someone they aren't. In these situations, as opposed to saying, "I can't be that woman for you" these women pretend as if they can, to get the man. Once they feel secure in the relationship, they fall off. It's imperative as singles that we know and own who we are during the dating and courting process. Don't be afraid to be your authentic self, even embracing the not so good parts of you. If you must jump through hoops or mask who you are just so a man can be attracted to you... is that what you really want? Being real with yourself, what pressures are you allowing, or have you allowed men to put on you to gain their interest?

Many women attest that 'A man has the capability to fool you, and you'll never truly know who a person really is' and I must agree that statement has some validity. However, the proclivity of that statement is determined by what you choose to see and what you are willing to know, accept, and put up with. Remember, wisdom is available to us if we ask for it. When's the last time you asked for wisdom concerning a guy you've dated or are dating? I'm not talking about that detailed prayer you've submitted including what you want and don't want in a man! We've all got what we've asked for and later found out, that wasn't truly what we wanted. No ma'am, I'm talking about lifting a specific person's name up in prayer and asking God to show you all of him. If you have done that and still experienced deception, I challenge you to look a little deeper. Were there occasions when you ignored the signs? God promises not to leave you ignorant, so that means, He will tell you if a person is for you or not. Ladies, if you want the truth, God's guidance, a true romantic relationship, and God's best for you, establish friendships. Never forgetting or neglecting to maintain your relationship with God as you experiment with potential suitors.

At one point in my life, I was queen of 'meet a man and two weeks later be madly in love'. However, through experience, I learned a better way of dating. After years of doing it all wrong I learned how trivial those decisions were and how detrimental a two-week fall-head-over- heels-in love-type of romance was to the longevity of any relationship and even to me. Early in my singleness when I was that desperate chick, I wanted a man's attention so much so that if a man (not just any man, you know my criteria) claimed me as his girlfriend or told me he loved me, despite me feeling the same way or not, I made myself love him back. I would become his girlfriend. I forced myself to like him and I chose to love him because, after all I was never confident that I would have the privilege to meet the man God had for me. Honestly, I wasn't even sure he existed.

In my desperation, a man could have told me five times over, "I don't want a relationship" I would still refuse to believe him. Simply because, we had sex and went out from time to time I was sure I had what it took to change his mind. I know many women who find themselves in this predicament today and because of my life experiences I am very sensitive to women and the choices they make concerning men. I have lived on every side of the fence as it relates to dating. Because of this I can find a level of compassion instead of judgement. In this instance ask yourself, "am I treating other women the way I want to be treated?" Through it all, I have learned the importance of setting boundaries and sticking to them, being confident in who I am as a woman and never letting a man dictate my life. This moment of transparency leads me to my next type of friendship.

Since we've discussed the importance of establishing a friendship first with a potential partner, let's talk about being friends with men who are interested in you, but you don't share the same sentiment. Let's be clear, this section is not about the male friend with whom you have set boundaries with. To be more specific, I'm talking about the "home boy" who has a girlfriend, fiancé, or wife (who is aware of your friendship), or the guy you've known since high school or college, or even a family friend, etc.

This section is dedicated to the guy who likes you romantically and you know without a doubt there will be nothing more than a friendship, however for selfish reasons you continue this relationship with him anyway... STOP IT. We know you reap what you sow. My suggestion to sever this "friendship" is backed up by the following argument. Ask yourself these two questions: What is the underlying purpose of that friendship and is this purpose in the best interest of both parties? Need further explanation... here it goes. Are you serious about having this friendship because it occupies your lonely times, it replaces an eluded companion, you benefit by receiving money or gifts, you have somebody to pay for something you don't feel like paying for, etc.? Are you using this man and slapping friendship on it, when it's convenient for you? After all, you reap what you sow. Honestly Sis, this tactic can be extremely manipulative and has the likelihood of ultimately labeling you as a user; a representation that isn't helpful for where you're going. Trust me you will carry those tendencies into your relationship and if not eradicated will lead to some serious, and might I add preventable issues. You'll begin the process of manipulating situations, so that they are advantageous for you. You'll become a person who has the habit of taking only what you want from people and giving far less, and in some cases, nothing at all. When you know good and well you have no intentions of being anything more than friends with a man, don't entertain him simply because he is nice, willing to be vulnerable, and pays you some attention (because no other man is), he doesn't need any favors. You don't want to begin an unhealthy relationship with one man as a filler until another one comes along and that phrase "I told him I only want friendship" does not cut it when the man starts treating you like you are more than his friend. That's called an opportunist and it speaks very negatively to your character. You don't want that Sis!

The *Single Committed Woman* understands the importance of cutting off relationships with guys who clearly do not understand plutonic friendship. When I became a *Committed Single Woman* for years I did not have any male friends.

Sure, I had some old coworkers or men that I spoke with during random encounters out and about but when I chose to be holistically single, it was important for me to monitor a man's motives before furthering communication. I quickly realized that while some men claimed to only want my friendship, some of them had horrible intentions. Ladies, you know when a man wants more from you than a conversation, and I'm not only talking about sex. Some men are lonely just like you, anxious just like you, needing validation just like you and because you are pretty, or nice, or that "good girl" (they think they want) they target you. You know when a man has intentions on winning you over, or influencing you to be with them. These men need to be removed because it breeds toxicity and chaos in your life. You may think they are filling a void or occupying a space, but in all actuality this person is really wasting your time and hindering your growth. Taking it to a whole new level, they are really a reflection of you.

Finally, I want to address the topic of married women who have male friends. I know this book is primarily for single women; however, for the married women reading and for you single ladies who will one day be married, this section is for you. Attention all my married girlfriends, it's simple...... you are married! If you are like most women when you were single, you were dying to be married so why are you longing for that single life again? Single women can have various male friends... you my married friend; need to do away with all male friendships that your husband has no idea about. Be careful not to play yourself; mentioning this "male friends" name a time or two to your husband is irrelevant if you talk to this "male friend" every day, accept gifts, money, favors, etc. from this guy. God forbid if you are having sexual relations with this man, you must stop. Like really, this is not a good practice of honoring yourself, family, and your vows. Everything about that relationship is unhealthy and does not serve you, especially in the long run. Trust me; these friendships almost always end up a hot mess! Your emotions become radical, your attitude starts to suck, everyone will suddenly start getting on your nerves, you'll experience feelings of unhappiness, confusion about everything, and this list can go on and on. Women who have male friendships in their marriage, unknown to their husband, are typically the same single woman who used men to her advantage during her singleness. Sorry Sis, but not sorry. The bottom line is this: If you have male friends in a marriage your husband needs to be just as friendly with this man, can contact him, and literally have as much access as you have to your male friend. Habits of a single woman are often perpetuated into a marriage without acknowledgment and a determination to change.

Stingy Single Girl

Now, we will talk about a sensitive topic, Giving. A woman who is a *Committed Single Woman* understands this concept too. I am unsure if you are aware or not but in a relationship, you will be doing much more giving than you were or are doing now as a single person. I am not only talking about money, (something that could be shared in a marriage) but your time, energy, and talents are all needed when you become a wife. Right now, while you are single, practice giving by taking advantage of all the facilities and organizations in your area that need your help. If you are a teenager, college student, or are unemployed, money may not be easily accessible for you, so be creative about ways you can give.

I experienced a stingy stage early in my singleness. As a teenager I was a giver. Oh, goodness thinking back if a classmate had a tragedy, or a person was picked on in school I rallied money and things from my house, even spending my earned cash to purchase items for the student or family in need. I found so much joy in giving, but when bills came that required my money I watched as my always open hands became tight like fists. So once God revealed that ugly part of me, I started to give again. Not bill money or anything like that but some of that extra cash I reserved for entertainment or a restaurant meal, I simply gave it away.

I figured I could sacrifice a movie, when I had cable and plenty of DVDs, or I could sacrifice a nice dining experience when I had groceries at home when there were people living without the slightest idea of how they would get their next meal. I began to ask God to show me who to give money to and even how much. Tithing was an area I chose to develop as well for many reasons. Tithing is an issue that many people fight against because they are tightfisted. If you are concerned that the pastor is misusing the money, you are not operating in wisdom by even going to that church, let alone paying a tithe there. God will not have you sow good seed into bad ground, nor will He want you to be a follower of a false prophet or a thieving pastor! One of the greatest attributes of a tither is their outward and inward demonstration of trust in God as a result of giving back a small percentage of their income to the expansion of His ministry, further creating good in the world. When someone tithes they are showing their willingness to trust God with their money. Adopting the attitude that tithing into ministry to further the good news or donating to help those in need is the primary reason for tithing. This message of giving ties into singleness because *The Committed Single* woman gives back and does so happily because she is honoring God; another one of those traits necessary to maximize your singleness. She also understands that by paying her tithe she is also practicing giving without receiving an immediate return. She is giving out of full faith that by doing the right thing everything else will work out in her favor. Please note tithing is not limited to giving to a church per say. Tithing can be giving a portion of your income to charity, the homeless, etc. Isn't that the proper attitude to have as you wait for the relationship God has for you? Isn't that the right way to handle your dating/courting relationships? Doing your part and trusting that God will do His? Additionally, when you pay a tithe or give for the good your confidence develops, and you begin to understand certain principles such as He will supply all your needs in exchange of your obedience. I was also challenged during my singleness to spread my tithes around to different ministries. If you are connected to a church I do not encourage that unless it's a message you received from God, but if you are still in search for the right church home, ministry or whatever ask God which ministries you need to sow your seeds. It could be an organization, an individual, a school, etc. if God leads you to give there, give. This signifies your obedience to Him and further validates for Him your willingness to obey. He's faithful.

A second area the *Committed Single Woman*

practices is giving her time. Be careful not to give your time as merely something to do, please be intentional about all your actions. Make sure when you are giving your time you do it with enthusiasm and for the benefit of the receiver. Not so you can brag, feel good about yourself, or to find something to occupy your time because a date canceled on you last minute. If you are unsure where to give your time, ask God. For starters, I am sure a great place to start is your neighborhood or community, a place you pass by often full of people who needs that attention.

Moreover, I know you have seen or heard the girls in your community who roam the neighborhood or hang on the corner near you. Have you ever thought about approaching that group of teens to try to know more about them? Have you considered introducing yourself to them? So many young people are just looking for love and attention and what better way to offer your time and love than to a lost young girl in your community. All it takes is some of your time and money for a lunch date, or mani-pedi appointment, something to practice the habit of giving and expecting nothing in return. You will be amazed at how you can change some girl's life by allowing her to run errands with you or help you volunteer at various places. Many of us as singles are smack dab in the middle of a gold mine, but we are busy trying to find our treasure in relationships and men. I've highlighted strangers as the one's we could share our time with, but many of us single women have family members that we have neglected. Brothers, sisters, nieces, cousins etc. that on a Friday night instead of trying to land a date we could call them up and talk to them about life goals, invite them over for a slumber party, or join them at a movie. They may gripe and complain about it, but that's just a front. These children love and appreciate time and attention and who are you kidding, you do too. Ladies work on giving in your singleness: there are so many schools that need volunteers, and small organizations that need a helping hand, where are you? Lost in your thoughts of this fantasy relationship, bound to a man that is long gone and moved on, living vicariously through the basketball wives or love & hip-hop lovers, wishing that so and so would return your calls or take you out tonight.... Please, the *Committed Single Woman* knows all that is foolishness and guards her heart against those useless emotions and thoughts.

You are Single There Are Good Times to be Had

Many people overlook the necessary areas that should be developed during singleness, but be careful not to forget the fun to be had as a single woman too. No one wants to be with a boring girl. I consider myself a homebody, but when it's time to have fun I know how to be the fun girl. I love to laugh, hang out with family and friends, dance, play games, I am not much of an outdoors girl, but I'll try it. All in all, I enjoy life and I love to experience new things. How many single friends do you have? Many people use this as a negative connotation, but not in this book. It's more beneficial to have many single friends than a whole bunch of unhappily married folks jading your image of marriage and relationships. Planting negative seeds of doubt in your head about your ability to get married or how they wish they were still single...etc., so you and your single gal pals have my vote! Anyway, back to the question at hand don't laugh or be ashamed... how many single gal pals do you have? Well, take those girls and start having fun! Plan date nights, Ladies Night Out, wine tasting trips, shopping parties, slumber parties, lunch dates, community service group activities, sip and paint excursions, vacays, etc. If you are already doing that, keep doing it with enthusiasm. I am not sure what lofty ideas you have about marriage, but you will be doing the same things, it will just be with you husband. I know many married women who long for a Ladies Night Out. Sure, you will be doing a little bit more with your husband, or at least I PRAY YOU WILL, who am I kidding if you are holding the goods until marriage the poor man is going to get worn out, Whoop! Whoop! But ladies come on, anything in life will get boring if you don't keep a positive attitude and add some PIZZAZZ to it. Exercise with your girlfriends, there are many things you can do with your girlfriends or your family and have a great time doing them during your singleness. Don't waste your life waiting for a relationship, what if one never comes?

What if your love life needs more time to flourish, perhaps several more years? You don't want to waste your time living life half way, holding onto a wing and a prayer when God has commanded you to enjoy the luxuries He has given you right now, at this moment! He knows what He's doing, no need to doubt that but, the question is do you know what you're doing? There is fun to be had with the people who want to be in your life and the people strategically placed there. Run from loneliness, it desires your thought life. It's on a mission to consume you with thoughts of doom and gloom. Accept the freedom and cling to what you have in your life, right now. Also learn to enjoy your own company. I believe people who can't stand to be by themselves are running from the responsibility of having to think about and analyze their lives. It's something about sitting alone that starts putting things into perspective. Helping you judge your actions (right, wrong or indifferent) and how you can adjust. Examining your words and how you use them. While these are just a few examples, the areas of your growth, or lack thereof, start to surface once you become isolated. Trusting God means that His will is the only plan for your life. This is a huge commitment. It's difficult when you grow up with all these fantasies about how you want your life to be. We all have those fantasies, often wrecked by reality! Initially, that feels like one of the most disheartening things you could ever experience because you have grown up believing that whatever you want is the best for you; not taking into consideration that sometimes what we're after is only the pursuit because fantasy is all we've been exposed to. I want to introduce the idea that because God is omnipotent even your greatest ideas could never compare to what He knows and has planned for your life. As a single woman, I have shared with you in more ways than one throughout this book, how it has truly been a struggle trusting God especially when you desire a love life so pure. I've been there, at one point in my life all a fine man had to do was wink at me and he had me. I was so desperate and unenlightened, not because I did not have the tools but because I did not want to do what was required! I wanted a husband and have wanted one since I was 12 years old. That's a long time. I really thought I was that girl who would be engaged by 18, married by 21, and having a kid the next year. Like I told you earlier, if I had married when I thought I should have I would have created a MESS. I would have destroyed both our lives. I'm so glad that today I can maturely thank God that He did not honor my requests. I know more people who got married at the age I thought I should have and are now divorced and others are struggling hard to make it through. I know people who were once high school sweethearts, who cannot stand to hear of, speak of, or think of the guy they were so madly in love with in the 12th grade. Having a successful marriage in our generation is possible, but it takes a level of commitment beyond ourselves that this peer group, hesitantly practices. As singles we can't start comparing our lives with others because they have something we want, or even make ourselves out to be better than someone because they have something we do not want. God has a plan for their life just like He has a plan for yours, and it's all for His purpose. Some single women had children with men who were/are the worst candidate for a father, but God has a way of taking our mistake and using them for His glory. For the single mothers, be encouraged, there is no way of knowing what type of damage your child(ren) may have shielded you from; toxic relationships, people, careers and so forth so be thankful for your blessing. God knows how to put road blocks in our plans and it's always for purpose. Trust God with your relationship status, honor Him with your commitment and let what you say to Him mean something. Practice patience and giving. Develop relationships with family and friends. Work on being a better you, and don't focus on what you do not have, celebrate what you do!

My Biggest Takeaway

As we end here, hopefully you were able to take on a new outlook concerning your relationship status and embark upon or continue your journey fiercely. With that, I want to encourage you. First, I want to thank you for taking the time to read this book. Not only was it therapeutic for me, my prayer is that it served as a refresher for you and that you recommend it to someone that may be refreshed by it as well. I've grown a lot from the time I first started this book to today. I discovered a lot about myself, my life, and my relationships that caused me to add, edit, and even replace parts of this book and for that I am grateful.

The process of writing this book truly highlighted my insecurities and opened a slew of knowledge to me, about me. I could turn my personal experiences into health or detriment. I uncovered so many undeveloped parts about myself including but not limited, to poor communication and leading with my emotions. I never considered how the circumstances I experienced in my life caused me to be drawn to arguments and fights and how I equated that to being loved. Or, how dishonest I was with men; masking my real intentions for desiring them, largely in part because I had no clue. I thought I could manipulate people into doing and being what I wanted them to be. I discovered my persistent quest of seeking approval from men and realized I had never affirmed myself or accepted God's affirmations of me. I found that I was willing to settle, just to say that I had someone rather than wait on the man I deserved, while secretly believing we'd never meet. I found that I thought my body was my only commodity. I found that I could tell everyone else about their relationships but could never apply the same advice to myself, and I'd make excuses for it. I found that I never really lived in the moment because I was always looking for the next big thing. I found that I was willing to commit to men who would never commit to me. Literally, giving my body to one man time after time, who would in return spiritually share me with all the other women he'd slept with. I learned that I never valued, understood, or even respected sex. I found that I had no idea who I really was, I just had an idea of who I wanted to be, and I'd present her initially to make people believe I was somebody I wasn't. I realized I was willing to do anything to make a man happy and never gave an ounce of consideration to my own happiness.

During my self-discovery I found that I really wasn't ready for a relationship. My quest for being a wife was heavily misguided and led me to many useless relationships, in the bed of men who were never my friends, and often men I was never in a relationship with, but I secretly tried to make my husband, which resulted in a long list of heartbreaks, and on-the-floor, head-to-the ground, crying my eyes out on several occasions type prayers. Just like it is with many sins and mistakes, I had a legitimate desire, to be a wife, but I defiled God and myself trying to attain that desire. I have been on every side of the spectrum and I get it. I get it, if your singleness has been a compete mess and I get it, if your singleness has been extremely rewarding to you. I get it, if you're in a dead-end relationship and I get it, if you're currently experiencing the sweetest love you've ever known. I get it, if your marriage is trash and if your marriage is harmonious. I get it! So, the entire purpose of this book is to inspire you. Help you realize that you hold the key to the success or failure of your relationships, no matter what stage you're in. How your singleness really colors your relationships and if the fundamental work is not done and the foundational process is omitted, single, dating or married you're setting yourself up for failure. The goal however, is not to fail. It is to become the best versions of ourselves and that goal can be attained. As a matter of fact, we can surpass that goal and lead very healthy lives and experience rewarding relationships. I hope this book equips you with the ammo to get started. Highlights areas for growth and helps you to understand where you are, where you came from and where you're going. You maximize your love life at any stage by being happy and progressive. You're going up baby and to say I am proud of you is an understatement. Keep God first and remain focused; your possibilities are limitless. May blessing overtake your life and may you experience a love so pure and true, in this life, and share your love with the world.

Let's Stay Connected

@konversations_w_kristen

konversationsk

konversationsk
www.konversationsk.com

9780999547502